THE SOCIAL GOD

THE AUTHOR

Kenneth Leech is a graduate of King's College, London and Trinity College, Oxford. He trained for the priesthood at St Stephen's House, Oxford and was ordained in 1964. He worked for several years in the East End of London and in Soho among drug addicts and wrote *A Practical Guide to the Drug Scene* which has been acclaimed as the best book written on the problems of drug dependence. He is also the author of *Youthquake*, a study of the '50s and '60s, *Soul Friend*, a study of spirituality, and *True Prayer*. From 1971–4 he was chaplain of St Augustine's College, Canterbury and was Rector of St Matthew's, Bethnal Green from 1974–80. Since 1980 he has been Race Relations Field Officer of the Church of England's Board for Social Responsibility. He is married with one son.

Kenneth Leech

THE SOCIAL GOD

First published
in Great Britain in 1981
by Sheldon Press
SPCK
Marylebone Road
London NW1 4DU

Thanks are due for permission to use copyright material from *Collected Poems* by John Betjeman published by John Murray (Publishers) Ltd, and Houghton Mifflin Company.

Typeset in Great Britain by
King's English Typesetters Limited, Cambridge
and printed in Great Britain by
Ebenezer Baylis and Son Ltd,
The Trinity Press, Worcester and London

ISBN 0 85969 342 2

Contents

Preface

This book grew out of lectures given to conferences and groups, or as articles in journals, during the past few years. All of them have been considerably expanded, revised or developed. They represent my thinking on a range of contemporary themes and issues, but the common thread which runs through them all is the conviction that there is an essential unity between contemplation and action, between prayer and politics, between the mystical and the prophetic dimensions of Christian life. There is no 'social gospel', as there is no 'spirituality', apart from the gospel itself: on the contrary, the Christian God is a social God, whose nature is social and who shares his nature with human kind. It is this belief which is the basis of this book.

Chapter 1 is based on a paper given to a group of Episcopalian clergy at Flossmore, Illinois, in October 1978. Chapters 2, 3, 4, and 9 originally appeared in shorter form as Jubilee Papers, and Chapter 3 was also published as an article in *Theology* in March 1976. Chapter 5 was originally prepared as a Lent Lecture at the University Hospital of Wales, Cardiff, but could not be given because of weather conditions: it was, however, included in a collection of papers published by the Church in Wales Publications in 1978.

Chapter 6 was given at a conference of young clergy in Chelmsford in 1974, but has been considerably expanded. Chapter 7 was a paper given at a conference of pastors and psychotherapists in 1978, and appeared in *Contact* 61 (1978).

Chapter 8 was given at a conference of the Consultative Council of Religious Communities at St Andrew's House, Notting Hill, in 1977. Chapter 10 was a lecture to the Christian Socialist Movement at the House of Commons in March 1978.

Chapter 11 is based upon a short article in *The Chosen Race*, a pamphlet published by the Student Christian Movement, but has been very much expanded. Chapter 12 was a paper given to the Jubilee Group in Cambridge, Massachusetts, in November 1979.

I am grateful for permission to reissue the papers in this form.

1
Christian Social Action: Its Theological Basis

The changing face of evangelicalism

The renewal of social concern among Christians in the West has been most marked in recent years among some evangelicals. In fact it might be seen as the central feature of the changed face of evangelical Christianity since the international Congress on World Evangelization at Lausanne in 1974. In the symposium on the Lausanne Covenant, published in 1976 under the title *The New Face of Evangelicalism*, there is great emphasis on this renewal. Thus René Padilla of the International Fellowship of Evangelical Students in Buenos Aires writes:'Christian social responsibility is given in the covenant a place of prominence that can hardly be regarded as characteristic of evangelical statements.' There was, he claims, a strong rejection of 'the unbiblical divorce between the kerygma and the diakonia'[1] Athol Gill, who has been connected with the Australian Radical Discipleship Group, saw the Lausanne Covenant as 'a turning point in evangelical thinking'. The Lausanne Covenant, however, was not alone, for in 1966 a congress at Wheaton had issued the Wheaton Declaration which proclaimed: 'We have sinned grievously. We are guilty of unscriptural isolation from the world that too often keeps us from honestly facing and coping with its concerns.' Again, the Declaration of Evangelical Social Concern which was signed at Chicago in 1971 called on evangelicals to attack American materialism and the maldistribution of the world's wealth and resources.[2] At Lausanne itself the Radical Discipleship Group, dissatisfied with the weak position taken by the Covenant, issued a statement denouncing as 'demonic' all attempts to drive a wedge between evangelism and social concern.[3]

It would, of course, be too optimistic and quite mistaken to see this shift in some evangelical circles as the only factor in the current scene. Alongside it must be placed the persistence of the individualist and pietist streams in evangelical thought and, in recent years, a revival of a type of reactionary and regressive pietism which is highly suspicious and critical of the changes mentioned above. Many evangelicals in Britain remain unaware of, or unaffected by, the changes in outlook. So one still finds much British evangelicalism allied with a conservative and even Erastian view of civil society, a view which is illustrated in the widespread support for the establishment of the Church of England.[4] Firmly rooted within the establishment, most evangelicals continue to operate with a working vocabulary from which not only such concepts as revolution and social change, but even such biblical themes as body, humanity and kingdom, are absent. Instead one finds innumerable references to the individual experience of the Christian. Moreover, the stress in most social protest movements of evangelical origin is on personal (particularly sexual) morality rather than on structural injustice, a notion which remains strange to most evangelicals. Apologies for social concern tend to be very disappointing and operate within a set of social and cultural assumptions which are not questioned.[5] Moreover, there has been a resurgence of a type of pietism which is both critical of what it sees as 'politicising' trends and also hostile to any real political commitment. This pietism, which is often linked with the Charismatic movement, may use a 'radical' vocabulary, but its main impact is towards quietism and support of the *status quo*.[6] Reactionary trends can be observed in the USA where there has been an upsurge of a very right-wing evangelical presence on television and in the 'born-again' movements of the white suburbs.[7] It is these groups who have helped to bring Ronald Reagan to power.

However, in spite of all these factors, there is no doubt that a new radical evangelical position is emerging in the west. It is important for Christians of all traditions because it is the most outstanding illustration of a commitment to social change which is rooted in biblical faith. Prominent in this new tendency are such figures as Ronald Sider,[8] John Howard Yoder,[9] and Jim Wallis and the Sojourners Community.[10]

These writers are most insistent on the biblical basis of their social concern. Sider, for example, claims that 'evangelicals are weak in social ethics because their theology is not sufficiently biblical'.[11] The Sojourners community has even been attacked for offering a 'fundamentalist social gospel' and the same unfriendly critic refers to them as 'political snake handlers'.[12]

Yet undoubtedly Sojourners represents a vigorous new force in the world of evangelical social thinking, and recent issues of its journal of the same name indicates its debt to Christian thinkers of other traditions such as the late Thomas Merton and Henri Nouwen, perhaps the leading Roman Catholic spiritual writer in the USA today. The biblical basis of Christian social action comes over very clearly in the writings of Jim Wallis, the founder and leading spokesman of the Sojourners group. Writing of the new evangelical radicals he says:

> This process of radicalization does not require the creation of a new theology or value system. It involves rather a return to biblical Christianity. However strong the opposition to the established order, however revolutionary the vision, the basic values and commitments are familiar to those acquainted with the biblical and historic traditions of the church. The startling thing about the insurgents is their affirmation of biblical faith, their sense of continuity with the radical Christian heritage of times past.[13]

In a review of Richard Quebedeaux's *The Young Evangelicals* (1974) Wallis observed of this new breed:

> It is a rediscovery of the demands of discipleship and a return to the biblical roots of faith. As such, unity comes from a common commitment to the Lordship of Jesus Christ as it is revealed in the Scriptures.[14]

From the days of the Lausanne Conference of 1974 through to the present, the Sojourners tendency has criticised the older evangelical mentality represented by such figures as Billy Graham. Commenting on Graham's address at Lausanne, in which he stressed the 'salvation of souls' over against social and political involvement, a member of the Sojourners group noted that there was 'a growing number of evangelicals, particularly from the Third World, who reject such a non-biblical simplistic separation of the "spiritual" from the "political"'[15] Writing more recently, Wallis stresses the rediscovery of the biblical understanding of the nature of the church as the essential prerequisite of renewal.

> The greatest need in our time is not simply for *kerygma*, the preaching of the gospel, nor for *diakonia*, service on behalf of justice, nor for *charisma*, the experience of the Spirit's gifts, nor even for *propheteia*, the challenging of the king. The greatest need of our time is for *koinonia*, the call to simply be the church – to love one another, and to offer our life for the sake of the world. The creation of living, breathing, loving communities of faith at the local church level is the foundation of all the other answers.
>
> Proclamation of the gospel, charismatic gifts, social action, and prophetic witness alone do not finally offer a real threat to the world as it is, especially when set apart from a community which incarnates a whole new order. It is the ongoing life of a community of faith that issues a basic challenge to the world as it is, and offers a visible and concrete alternative. The church must be called to be the church, to rebuild the kind of community that gives substance to the claims of faith.[16]

Very much in line with the thinking of the Sojourners group is the concern, expressed in the recent study by Jeremy Rifkin and Ted Howard,[17] for a 'second Reformation' involving commitment to radical social change.

In Britain, the impetus for the movement of evangelicals towards a deeper understanding of the social character of the Gospel came mainly as a byproduct of urban ministries in several British cities. The influence of David Sheppard, now Bishop of Liverpool, has been a significant and continuing one. In his study *Built as a City* (1974) Sheppard described the changes in his own theology as a result of his inner-city experience. While his position remains very conservative and cautious in many respects, it does represent a major advance from conventional Anglican evangelical approaches.[18] The work of evangelical social activists such as Denis Downham in

Spitalfields in the early 1960s, while it did not directly affect thinking, helped to create an atmosphere in which social action by biblical Christians became respectable, and it therefore cleared the ground for later, more radical developments.[19] Since the early '60s there has been a marked change in evangelical social attitudes. Writing in 1972, David Moberg subtitled his book *The Great Reversal* 'Evangelism versus Social Concern', a polarisation which the author himself went on to reject as unbiblical.[20] Today more evangelicals are tending, with Sider, to see evangelism and social justice as equally important concerns for God's people. It is increasingly common for evangelicals to stress that 'the general awakening of the church to its full maturity within history will not occur without the conjunction of piety and justice in its laity and its leadership.'[21]

It is encouraging too to find evangelical journals such as *Third Way* publishing criticisms of the individualistic bias of earlier attitudes. So a writer in 1977 stressed that the centre and interest, the weight of gravity, in the Bible is not in the fate and destiny of the individual, but rather in the renewal of creation and the coming of the Kingdom.[22] More recently a writer in the same journal attacked evangelical pietism.

> Salvation for evangelicals takes place in the realm of the cosmic spirits or in the inner realms of human conscience. Conversion happens when one claims to believe in Jesus' atonement and then feels forgiveness and inner peace. Becoming a Christian is not seen to require any fundamental changes such as an acceptance of particular ways of behaving both inwardly and corporately that become an alternative to the broader society. One can become an evangelical Christian and still be a racialist, for example. In America, sociologists Glock and Stark have demonstrated that the more seriously Americans take their church membership, the more racist and patriotic they are, and the less capable of loving their enemies.[23]

By contrast, the new breed of evangelical places a more truly biblical emphasis on the Kingdom of God and on the social dimensions of salvation.

The doctrinal basis of social action

I have devoted considerable space to the changes in the evangelical world because it is here that the roots of social action in Christian doctrine are most clearly stressed. But the changed atmosphere here is only one facet of a new concern in various parts of the Christian world for what I will call *social theology*, that is, for a social concern which is not merely an 'implication' of, a secondary byproduct of, Christian faith, but which is integral to that faith. I shall argue that there is in fact no 'social gospel' apart from *the* Gospel, a Gospel which is *essentially* social. I want to approach this question by examining the nature of the church, and I shall do this under three heads. First, the church as itself social, a society rooted in the social being of God. Secondly, the church as servant, a popular, though I shall suggest, misused term. Thirdly, the church as prophetic minority and herald of the Kingdom of God. I want to draw on the basic theology of our concern with society, and to look at the biblical basis for this concern.

I suggest that it is vital that we begin with the nature of God and with revelation. Christianity is essentially social and essentially involved. It is social because God is social, and it is involved because God is involved. There is no such thing as a purely personal Gospel, and there is no such thing as an uninvolved theology – or, if there is, it is not Christian theology. God is social and God is involved: that truth was crucial to the debates with heresy in the first four hundred years of the church's life. The doctrine of the Trinity is essentially the assertion of the social nature of God. So that great Anglican socialist priest, Conrad Noel, founder of the Catholic Crusade, could begin his book *Jesus the Heretic* (1939) with a chapter on 'The Blessed Trinity as the Basis of a New World Order'. Noel wrote:

> Let us then consider the Blessed Trinity as the source of our own personal lives and of the life of the world. Each one of us is a trinity in unity – body, mind and spirit: the disunity between these is not according to the original intention of the Triune God. The world has in it plenty of variety, but the variety is not always healthy, is often antagonistic and discordant, because it is not a variety in unity, and does not yet express the 'Three in One and One in Three'. It cannot

> be said of the world, as at present constituted, that it contains no differences or inequalities, or that within it 'none is afore or after other; none is greater or less than another'. We look forward to a world of infinite variety in harmony, of living unity, not, of dead uniformity; if man is to create so delightful a world, he 'must thus think of the Trinity', for it is the will of the Triune God to inspire men to renew the world in such a way as to make it the perfect expression of his own Being.[24]

In language strikingly similar to that used by Noel in the 1930s, a recent study by Mar Ostathios of the Syrian Orthodox Church in India emphasises 'the Trinitarian basis of social justice.'

> How can we follow the co-equality of Father, Son and Holy Spirit in a society which is based on capitalism and class structures? The quest of our age is for socialism, classlessness, egalitarianism, equality of opportunity, equality in spite of all distinctions, and a world brotherhood in the model of the Holy Trinity . . . The basis of this classless society is not Marxism but the eternal love of the Holy Trinity in eternal action which nullifies inequalities and creates an essential equality without discarding distinctions. Christian revelation is the basis of such a classless society.[25]

Christian social action then is based upon the doctrine of God. The doctrine of the Trinity is an assertion that within the Godhead itself there is society and equality of relationship and that humanity is called to share in that divine life. Against the Arian heretics, the church insisted that God could and did share his nature with man, that we might be 'sharers in the divine nature' (2 Peter 1:4). The Arian god, on the other hand, was lonely, remote and uninvolved, and did not share his nature with man because he could not. His relationship with man was that of a tyrant to his slaves, and St Athanasius drew a connection between this theology of the Arians and their oppression of the poor. The Arian god was and is an uninvolved god, a god who is anti-social and removed from the affairs of earth. And let us not make the mistake of thinking that Arianism is dead. It is probably the established religion of Britain and America. 'God is not dead – he just doesn't want to get involved': that is the Arian god. He doesn't get involved because he cannot: his nature is incommunicable, it cannot be shared. The Arian world is a world marked at all points by separation: its theology denies relationships within the Godhead, between God and man, and between man and man. The doctrine of the Holy Trinity, the Social God, asserts both relationship and equality, in heaven and on earth.

The Christian God then is social and deeply involved. The doctrine of the Incarnation is that this God took to himself human flesh: that he raised manhood into God. To believe this is dangerous and controversial, and it is a total rejection of the view of God with which most people in the west work. For belief in the Incarnation is a rejection of the idea of God as a remote object, far removed from earthly concerns. The Incarnation is the basis of Christian social concern, the heart of Christian materialism. 'The Word became flesh' (John 1:14). It is essential to grasp how central is this insistence on the taking flesh of Christ to all Christian thinking. It is the earliest diagnostic test of spirituality in the Christian church (1 John 4:2). Everything hinges upon it: in Tertullian's words, it is on the flesh that salvation hinges.[26]

Now I want to go further and argue that the Church is rooted in the being of this social God who took to himself flesh. For the Church is, in St Paul's terminology, the *soma Christou*, the body of Christ. It is an organism, united with the living God in the most intimate manner, and its nature derives from God's nature. The Church is social and involved because God is social and involved. And we go on to say that the Church is one, holy, catholic, and apostolic. It is one, because in Christ the division of the human race is overcome. We become one man in Christ (Gal. 3.28). It is significant that the Greek word used for the pouring out of the Spirit at Pentecost, *diamerizomenai*, is the same word used of the scattering of the nations in the Book of Deuteronomy (Acts 2.3; Deut. 32.8). So the Holy Spirit reverses the chaos of Babel. Again, the Church is holy, because God is holy. But this holiness is to be expressed in communion, a totally new concept. For in Old Testament categories, that which is holy could not be common, for the two terms were contradictory. Yet in the Christian Church we have this revolutionary notion of 'holy communion'. The Church too is to be catholic, a much misused term. It does not mean universal. *Kat'holou* means wholeness, inner wholeness, completion. That which is catholic is that which is moving towards the fullness of God. St John Chrysostom defines the Church as 'the fullness of Christ'[27] and St Cyril of Jerusalem defines catholicity as completion.[28] It is thus the opposite of sectarianism, of racism, of all that divides mankind. Finally, the Church is apostolic. It is rooted in the apostles' doctrine, fellowship (*koinonia*), eucharistic life, and prayers (Acts 2.42).

The Church then is a society whose origins lie in the nature of God himself. It is his body, it is *soma Christou*. John Robinson[29] rightly says that the notion of 'the body' is 'the keystone of Pauline theology'. Against the world of the flesh, *sarx*, is set that of the redeemed, renewed, body, *soma*, the body of the resurrection. Baptism into Christ begins the process of creation of this new body, and the Eucharist, the breaking of the bread, is the sign of that new body. In the Eucharist we share in the nature of Christ whose body we both eat and are. As St Leo the Great says, 'the body of the man who is reborn in Christ becomes the very flesh of Christ'. To quote a contemporary Episcopalian writer: 'Through the Eucharist we are extensions of Christ's vulnerability, sustained by the food of his victory: we are not guards placed at the door of his anteroom to protect him from profanation or contact with the world.'[30]

In the past Anglicans in the Catholic tradition have seen the closest connection between the common life and sharing of the Eucharist and the social concerns of the world. Thus Bishop Frank Weston addressed the Anglo-Catholic Congress in 1923 in stirring words:[31]

> . . . the one great thing that England needs to learn is that Christ is found in and amid matter – Spirit through matter – God in flesh, God in the sacrament. But I say to you, and I say it with all the earnestness I have, that if you are prepared to fight for the right of adoring Jesus in his Blessed Sacrament, then you have got to come out from before your Tabernacle and walk, with Christ mystically present in you, out into the streets of this country and find the same

> Jesus in the people of your cities and villages. You cannot worship Jesus in the Tabernacle if you do not pity Jesus in the slum . . . And it is folly, it is madness, to suppose that you can worship Jesus in the Sacraments and Jesus on the throne of glory, when you are sweating him in the souls and bodies of his children . . . Go out and look for Jesus in the ragged, in the naked, and in the oppressed and sweated, in those who have lost hope, in those who are struggling to make good. Look for Jesus. And when you see him, gird yourselves with his towel and try to wash his feet.

The Church as servant

I now want to turn to the theme of the Church as servant, a theme which was very much at the centre of Bishop Weston's famous speech. The Church is to wash the feet of Christ in the poor and oppressed of the world. In our day the idea of 'the servant Church' became very popular in the 1960s as a result of a famous passage in Dietrich Bonhoeffer's *Letters and Papers from Prison* which was quoted by John Robinson in *Honest to God*, and thence entered the spirituality of the '60s.[32] Bonhoeffer said:[33]

> The church is her true self only when she exists for humanity . . . She must take her part in the social life of the world, not lording it over men, but helping and serving them. She must tell men, whatever their calling, what it means to live in Christ, to exist for others.

So we see the Church as the servant of humanity. As Christ took the form of a servant, so must we.

I want, however, to suggest that the scriptural basis for the view of the Church as servant needs more careful examination than it usually gets. It is essential to recognize that in many of our English Bibles the word 'servant' translates two quite distinct Greek words *doulos* and *diakonos* which have different meanings. In the Old Testament, the 'Servant of the Lord' (*Ebed Yahweh*) assumes a prominent place in Second Isaiah, and the 'suffering servant' passage in Isaiah 53 has been used a great deal by Christians. But the word servant here means slave: it is *doulos*, the slave of God, not of the world. In the New Testament, *doulos* is applied both to Christ and to Christians, though not directly to the Church, but it denotes slavery to God, not service to the world. The slave is one who has no rights, who is bound to God, his *Kurios*, his Master and Lord.

The other word is *diakonos*, servant. It is one of a group of 'service' words which have come into general use: others include *therapeuein* and *leitourgein*, from which we derive 'therapy' and 'liturgy'. *Diakonein*, to serve, occurs 34 times in the New Testament, while *diakonia*, service, occurs 31 times (though only in Luke in the Gospels), and *diakonos*, a servant, 28 times. The *diakonos* is one who serves tables (Luke 22.27), and in the famous passage in Mark 10.45 the Son of Man is said to have come in order to serve. (Note that *doulos* occurs in verse 44, while in verse 45 service, *diakonia*, is closely linked with suffering and sacrifice.) Paul uses *diakonia* with reference to the collection and support of Christian brethren and poor relief (Rom. 15.31, etc.). In 1 Corinthians 12, *diakonia* is listed as one of the spiritual gifts (12.5) and in Ephesians 4 there is a similar reference to the 'work of *diakonia*' (4.12). In all these references, however, service is within the Church, not from Church to world. Even the oft-quoted passage in Matthew 25 Inasmuch as you did it to one of the least of these . . . seems not to have referred originally to the service of humanity, but to the treatment *by* the world of the disciples, the little ones who follow Christ. The *diakonos*, servant or minister, in the New Testament is primarily one who serves the Church.

Perhaps the most interesting passage in the Epistles in which the concept of service is used is 2 Corinthians 5.18–20. Christ has reconciled the world to himself, and has entrusted to us the *diakonia* of reconciliation. Here is a twofold claim. First, the reconciliation wrought by God in Christ is for the whole world, not simply for the Church. Secondly, the ministry of reconciling is entrusted to the Christian community. Here the link is made between the Church and the world, but it should be noted that it is specifically connected with the ministry of reconciliation. In the same passage the term 'word (*logos*) of reconciliation' is used. Service and proclamation are not to be separated.

What I am suggesting is that the notion of the Church as the servant of the world does not find support in the New Testament in quite the way that is often thought. The primary task of the Church *vis-à-vis* the world is to confront it and to preach to it. It is striking that in the vast majority of the seventy-six uses of the word 'gospel' in the New Testament, the verb going with it is 'to preach', and preaching in the New Testament always refers to the proclamation of the gospel to the non-Christian world, not to the converted.[34] On the other hand, wherever 'service' is mentioned, the reference is almost always to the Church. The Church is certainly seen as a body which visibly manifests the gifts of the Spirit, a body where love is practised, a body to which humanity can look for evidence of a new life-style. But originally the link was indirect.

The development of the concept of service to include the idea of serving the needs of mankind was an inevitable and legitimate growth from taking the Incarnation seriously.[35] From the fact that one recognized the Son of Man in the faces of the poor of the world, St John Chrysostom can refer to the 'sacrament of the brother'. Yet there are two serious dangers in taking the servant concept as an adequate symbol for the Church's social concern. First, it can easily lead to the idea of a 'welfare church' and to 'social service religion'. Many years ago the great spiritual writer Evelyn Underhill referred to the trend towards a religion which stressed service at the expense of awe, 'a type of religion which in practice does not wear well'. 'I do not think we can deny', she wrote in 1953, 'that there is a definite trend in the direction of religion of this shallow social type.'[36] The second danger is that the servant church becomes the subservient church. Thus Martin Luther King, in one of his sermons, strongly denies that the Church is called to be the servant of the state. Still less is she to be its master. Her role is to be its conscience.[37]

This brings me to my next main point. In the New Testament the Church does not primarily exist to serve the world but to preach to it and to challenge its entire life and values. Today the servant Church is in danger of obscuring and replacing the prophetic church. Yet for the Bible, caring is not enough. Biblical social concern is not simply with helping casualties on the Jericho Road, but with the building of a new highway and a new city. The building of the new order of things, the Kingdom of God, is the work of God and we are called into collaboration with this work. It is this sense of a new world coming which drives and motivates the prophets.

Prophecy and the kingdom

Now prophecy is always a by-product of vision. A well-known Old Testament scholar has rightly noted that 'the prophets are frequently called "seers", never "hearers"'.[38] So the recovery of prophecy is essentially linked with vision, clarity of perception, spiritual discernment. One of the gravest threats to our social witness is partial vision. We are often too close to the needs of the world to see them clearly. We share in the diminished level of consciousness which is all around us, and where there is no vision the people perish. The recovery of Christian vision is essentially linked with the deepening of prayer and the life of the Spirit. Without that deep spirituality and contemplation, our social concern will be at best superficial tinkering, and at worst positively harmful to men and women.

Christian social action then is rooted in the being of God, in the saving events of the past, in incarnation, cross, and resurrection, but it is also oriented to the future. We seek a better City, the City that is coming, the City with foundations whose Builder and Maker is God (Heb. 13.14; 11.10.) It was as a result of their glimpse of the glory of God that the prophets thundered against social injustice, warned of impending doom, and proclaimed the coming of the New Age of God's justice. If the church is to recover its prophetic witness and is to challenge the values of a fallen world-order, it will only be as a by-product of its vision of God and its commitment to the Kingdom as the regulative principle of its theology.[39] In the New Testament, the combination of struggle and vision with service is contained in this dominant symbol of the Kingdom. Today we often hear what passes as the gospel preached without reference to the Kingdom. Yet the recovery of a Bible-based theology of the Kingdom of God is central to true Christian social concern. For 'we are looking for new heavens and a new earth, the home of justice' (2 Pet. 3.13).

If we are to recover an authentic theology of social action, it is vital to recover the centrality of the Kingdom of God. It is in the symbol of the Kingdom that the social being of God finds its earthly form and expression. The Kingdom is God manifested in earthly society. Yet so much modern 'Christian' preaching, Catholic and Protestant, reduces the Kingdom to an interior experience, or projects it into a remote future. Today the church is called to return to that essentially Jewish vision of the Kingdom as the New Age which is to transform and renew the face of the earth. In this return to a more truly biblical faith will be found the source of a dynamic Christian social action.

2
Catholic Theology and Social Change

Social dimensions of Catholicism

Catholic theology, like society itself, is changing, and within the broad spectrum of western Catholicism there are widely differing and contradictory elements and emphases. I want here to look at the western Catholic tradition as a whole, and only briefly at the Catholic movement within Anglicanism. Today, the Roman Communion might be compared – as the seventeenth-century Latitudinarian Cudworth compared the Church of England – to Noah's Ark, for it contains almost every kind of animal. Within this fold are both Marcel Lefebvre and the Berrigan brothers, the Warriors of Christ the King in Spain and Christians for Socialism in Chile. The range of social action includes the defence of established structures of oppression, and social rescue work within them, as well as Marxist and anarchist groups, movements of non-violent protest, fighters for racial justice, anti-abortion campaigners, radical feminists, and so on. All of these will claim to draw on some resources within Catholic theology. While Camillo Torres held that the Catholic who was not a revolutionary was in a state of mortal sin, many of the supporters of the Tridentine Mass see 'reds under the bed' even within the walls of the Vatican.

However, while this wide range will continue to exist, it is the official liturgical texts which will shape the future ethos of Catholic Christianity, for *lex orandi, lex credendi*, the rule of worship is the rule of belief. The new Roman Missal and Breviary form the daily worship of the Church, and the changes in emphases since the recent revisions are striking. The Vatican document *Gaudium et Spes*, frequently quoted in the readings in the Office, sees the Church as a serving church, and its service is in the cause of 'a new humanity', 'a new humanism'.[2] Gone is the old language of the 'supernatural order' – in fact, the word 'supernatural' is scarcely used in the Vatican texts at all. Instead we read of such concepts as integral development, man as the centre and crown of all things, the universal destination of the world's goods. Social action is based on social theology. Again, the collects of the Missal are concerned to stress the social nature of the Eucharist of the people of God, and it is this language which replaces the language of the Council of Trent. The intercessions at Evening Prayer in the new Breviary have a strong social flavour, referring to 'a community where justice and peace may flourish', prayer that 'human rights and freedom may be everywhere respected, and the world's resources may be generously shared', that the work of man may not disfigure the creation, and so on. There is a reduction in judicial and pietistic language, though the elements of prophecy and conflict are not apparent. The servant church seems to have replaced the prophetic church. The world is to be cared for and served, not to be challenged and renounced.

Now in principle some kind of social action based on Catholic theology was to be expected. For Catholic theology possesses certain characteristic features which would tend to lead in that direction, other factors being equal. First, Catholic theology is social theology, rooted in the theme of redemption for the world and for human society. This is not a discovery of Vatican II. The essentially social character of the teaching of the Catholic fathers was the central theme of Henri de Lubac's important work *Catholicism*, published in 1938. 'In reality', claimed de Lubac, 'Catholicism is essentially social . . . first and foremost in itself, in the heart of its mystery, in the essence of its dogma.'[3] It is crucial to the writings of the early fathers, and their writings were greatly used by the Catholic socialists of the nineteenth-century Anglican revival. Charles Marson claimed that the socialism of the early fathers was 'in exact proportion to their orthodoxy',[4] while Conrad Noel, the 'Red Vicar' of Thaxted, used to plaster his walls at theological college with quotations, apparently from extreme left-wing sources, and later revealed their source in Irenaeus, Basil, Ambrose, and John Chrysostom.

The work of Marson and Noel is typical of a whole school of Catholic Anglicans who saw the closest link between orthodox trinitarian and incarnational doctrine, and the struggle for social justice and equality.

Catholic theology is materialistic, rooted in the crude materialism of incarnation and sacraments, and totally opposed to the false spiritualizing of both. Adrian Hastings has written:

> True Christian moral commitment is a passionate concern with the particular and the material. Its grounding is in the particularity, the historicity, the materiality of Incarnation, Resurrection and Eucharist. The spiritualists and the demythologizers, for all their sincerity and all their devotion, hold to a different Christ and a different Gospel. Their spiritual resurrections and communions have no power to overturn the world of flesh, the segregation of race, the torture of the body. It is the risen flesh of the Incarnate Lord sacramentally present in the Eucharist which transforms a spiritual philosophy into a revolutionary creed.[5]

Thirdly, Catholic theology is an inclusive theology, wide, rich, deep, and open to development and growth. Stewart Headlam and his followers in the Guild of St Matthew stressed this facet and contrasted it with the restricting, narrow, and elitist nature of sectarianism.

Now it would be dangerous to make a simple causal link between Catholic theology and specific commitment to social change. Many other factors – class, cultural influences, and so on – are involved. But in principle Catholic theology is likely to lead to some kind of social action within the world, unlike Lutheran theology, for example, which contains within itself a violent separation of the material and spiritual kingdoms. The thinkers of the Christendom Group in the '30s – Reckitt, Demant, Peck, and the young Mascall – were partly correct in claiming that what they called Catholic sociology was deducible from Catholic dogma.[6] Catholicism is incompatible with a totally irresponsible attitude to human society; it cannot assume a wholly other-worldly posture. Nor in fact has the Catholic tradition been content with a social caring or ambulance role, although this aspect has been evident certainly since the time of Gregory the Great. At the centre of the Catholic view has been the vision of the City of God which is, in Augustine's words, 'partly seated in the course of these declining times . . partly in that solid state of eternity'.[7] The vision was of a unified society, directed towards the vision of God, a renewed creation, and this vision has remained in spite of the most severe distortions of the tradition.

The Vatican and its social outlook

The changing emphasis of Catholic social thinking can be seen in the 'social encyclicals' which were initiated by Leo XIII's *Rerum Novarum* of 1891. Written against the background of 'the spirit of revolutionary changes', Pope Leo did not welcome them. In fact, he reads like a nineteenth-century version of Archbishop Coggan, speaking of 'crafty agitators', and condemning socialism, class war, and the various subversives who were threatening the stability of the Christian order.[8] Pius XI's *Quadragesimo Anno* of 1931 reiterated the themes of its predecessor, stressing the rights of property, and condemning 'Christian socialism' as incompatible with Christianity. The most extreme of the papal documents of this period was the encyclical *Ingravescentibus Malis* of 1937 which urged the recitation of the Rosary as an anti-Communist weapon, to 'rout these subverters of Christian and human culture'. This was the period when, dominated by the fears of Communism, the Latin Catholic *bloc* took sides in the class war against the workers, and allied itself with Fascism and reaction. So we have Pius XI's concordat with Mussolini, the long alliance between the Roman Church and the Christian Democrats in Italy, the support of Franco and his followers ('dearest sons of Catholic Spain'), and the silence on Nazism on the grounds that 'the Pope is the Father of all the near and remote victims and culprits'.[9] In Italy, the use of Catholic Action to ensure the victory of the Christian Democrats has been a major factor in the decay of a true Catholic social conscience. Hastings comments:

> Pollution, shanty towns, appalling town planning, the particularly disgusting state of the city of Rome, cholera, the decay of Venice, the Mafia, the decline of the south, hamstrung educational and medical systems – the list of

> Italy's current and crying social ills could be continued almost indefinitely, to say nothing of what has now become a state of almost continuous political paralysis. And where, amidst all these crucial human and social needs, has the Church exerted her weight: To prevent legal divorce and contraception. Really the mind boggles.[10]

It is not simply the loss of any sense of perspective, but the apparent loss of vision of what is actually going on in the real world, which is so disturbing here. So in Italy, the Catholic social witness is often reduced to opposition to legal abortion, while the country continues to show one of the highest abortion rates in the world.

Throughout the entire period, the radical Catholic social voice was not totally silent. There were the nineteenth-century Catholic modernists, there was James Connolly and the Irish rebels of 1916, there was resistance to Franco from the Basque Catholics, and to Nazism from the French Catholic Left. There was the important influence of Jacques Maritain, and the Catholic anarchism of Peter Maurin, Ammon Hennacy, Dorothy Day, and the remarkable Catholic Worker collective in the USA.[11] It was in fact out of years of Catholic social thinking that there emerged in the '60s the encyclicals *Mater et Magistra* (1961) and *Pacem in Terris* (1963), the former dealing with 'socialisation', the latter with the issues of human rights, justice, equality, disarmament, migration, and so on. Pope Paul carried on from the social teaching of his predecessor, John XXIII. So *Populorum Progressio* (1967), denounced by the *Wall Street Journal* as 'souped-up Marxism', included the strongest condemnation of international capitalism and ignited the fires of revolutionary theology in Latin America. *Octogesima Adveniens* (1971), ironically issued on the thirtieth anniversary of *Rerum Novarum*, reduced its critique of socialism to the view that it was not 'a complete and self-sufficient picture of man', while Marxism was said to be a doctrine and method which furnishes some people not only with a working tool, but also 'a certitude preliminary to action: a claim to decipher in a scientific manner the mainsprings of the evolution of society'.[12]

Nevertheless, while the general direction of the Vatican's

social outlook has altered, there are still a number of distinct and conflicting theologies present in the Catholicism of post-Vatican II. The old authoritarianism is still clearly there, as the recent disputes over the Latin rite have shown. Pope Paul brought together in his own actions the curious mingling of progressive and reactionary elements which seems likely to characterize the present papal regime. The same Pope who issued *Populorum Progressio*, in the same year, visited the shrine at Fatima, 'a devotion which subtly reinforced the political pattern of Salazarism'[13] just as in 1944 Cardinal Griffin, in the context of the same cult, had broadcast to Portugal, and hailed her as the key nation who would bring Europe back to Christ. Pope John Paul II, in the year 1979, both encouraged the radicals at Puebla with his reassertion of the principle of the Medellin Conference, and left the North American progressive Catholics very disappointed indeed.[14]

With the Lefebvre movement and the upsurge of ecclesiastical conservatism, we see the surfacing of some very old and unpleasant aspects of Catholic social action. It is alarming that many observers have seen this phenomenon as merely liturgical, and ignored its close association with the resurgence of the Catholic extreme Right. In his famous sermon at Lille, Lefebvre, the former supporter of Marshal Pétain and opponent of universal suffrage, praised the junta in Argentina for their crushing of anarchy, and later added his praise for the regime in Chile. His supporters include many who saw Salazar as the nearest to a Christian society, and for whom Mussolini and Franco were a shade too liberal.[15] The new Catholic Fascism, like its predecessor, exalts order at the expense of freedom, opposes change, urges a return to the stable forms of the past, and fears the spectre of Communism which it sees everywhere.

On the other hand, tucked away in the pages of *Populorum Progressio*, was a small section which, while it advised against revolution, accepted its legitimacy by applying to it the old Catholic principle of the *justum bellum* – that a revolution was unjust if greater misery would be produced afterwards than existed before.[16] It was no doubt meant as a red light, but for the Catholics of Latin America, who were already in the midst of a revolutionary situation, it was the green light. Inspired by the encyclical, the Medellin Conference in 1968 issued guidelines for Catholic radicals in the Third World, and the 'liberation theology' which has emerged from Latin America is still in its early stages.[17] It represents a renewal of Catholic social theology, and a break with the false spirituality which has pushed the hope of the Kingdom into the next world. With St Bernard, it sings of 'the peace that is from heaven, and shall be too for earth', sentiments which we are now inclined to sing – it is Hymn No. 495 in the *English Hymnal* – with a spirituality which St Bernard never intended.[18]

Anglican Catholics and social change

What of Anglicans in all this ferment? In one sense, Anglicans are on the fringe of all the present movements, although much of the writing of the liberation theologians is reminiscent of the nineteenth-century Catholic socialists. Anglo-Catholicism has a mixed history as far as social action is concerned. While it is true that 'the radicalism of the original leaders of the movement is fairly easy to document'[19] the radical stage did not last long. The Catholic socialists – Headlam, Hancock, Marson, Noel and the rest – were always a tiny and atypical minority. Certainly there were strong elements of social concern in Bishop Weston's famous speech at the 1923 Anglo-Catholic Congress when he urged his hearers to 'come out from before your tabernacles. You cannot claim to worship Jesus in the tabernacle if you do not pity Jesus in the slum . . . If you say that an Anglo-Catholic has a right to hold his peace while his fellow-citizens are living in hovels beneath the level of the streets, then I say to you, that you do not know the Lord Jesus in his sacrament'.[20] But that kind of language was soon to fade, and many have used the material improvements since 1945 as excuse for evading the task of identifying the wounds of Jesus in the new poor. Today little is left of the social radicalism of the Anglo-Catholic tradition, and the reasons for this are complex. I will simply suggest four as pointers to further examination.

There was published in 1933 a large volume edited by the late N. P. Williams entitled *Northern Catholicism*, which put forward the thesis that there was a Catholic ethos peculiar to the countries of Northern Europe, a kind of spiritual regionalism.[21] While the purpose of the book was an eirenical and by no means narrow one, there were some results arising from its influence which were quite different. Williams and his colleagues were seeking to demonstrate the existence and validity of a non-papal Catholicism; they wished to encourage and strengthen the development of an indigenous Catholic life within the European traditions. However, their divorce of *Anglican* Catholicism from Rome had the effect of encouraging an independence and conservatism which was as hostile to social change as to liturgical change. Linked with this tendency was the growth of a stress on correctness and on the 'Englishness' of Catholic life. So there grew up the 'religion of taste' of which St Mary's Bourne Street became a symbol. Here Anglicans, Catholic and yet independent of, and unaffected by, Roman changes, cultivated a Catholic ethos which was aesthetically pure, socially and culturally genteel, and politically conservative. At Williams's own cathedral, Christ Church Oxford, the liturgy is still offered in the perfect style of the Anglicanism of 1933. This combination of social conservatism and archaic liturgical propriety as marks of Anglicanism is even more marked in some sections of the Episcopal Church of the USA.[22]

Again, while the emphasis of *Northern Catholicism* was on the European context of Catholic life, the stress on non-papal Catholicism tended to become linked with a kind of nationalism which associated Anglo-Catholicism with the Union Jack and with John Bull. While the nostalgia for 'Merrie England' was also combined with the Catholic socialism of Noel and the Thaxted movement,[23] it was more common to find it linked with a type of Catholicism from which the struggles of the contemporary world and the issues of social justice were far removed.

Closely linked with this first development, Anglo-Catholicism has become more and more absorbed into the bourgeois and largely Erastian culture of 'middle Anglicanism'. The identification of church and nation has a long pedigree in Anglicanism. Richard Hooker, for example, claimed that 'there is not any man of the Church of England, but the same man is also a member of the Commonwealth, nor any man of the Commonwealth which is not also of the Church of England'.[24] But, writing in 1933, the late C. B. Moss claimed that, whatever divisions might exist within the Catholic movement, all should agree that Erastianism was incompatible with Anglo-Catholicism. It was, said Moss,

> unhesitatingly rejected by all Anglo-Catholics alike as utterly incompatible, in modern conditions, with the religion of Christ. . . . This is an issue of life or death, not only for Anglo-Catholicism, but for spiritual religion of every kind.[25]

Nevertheless, the subsequent history of the movement has led to a reluctance to challenge the established order in civil society. This has coincided with the decline of Catholic prophecy and of Catholic spirituality, neither of which are happy bedfellows with conventional Anglicanism.

The Catholic movement in Britain and in the USA has tended, particularly since the 1950s, to become an ecclesiastical ghetto, marked by fear of change and by a defensive posture. Ecclesiastical conservatism has become associated with political conservatism and with the old order. Richard Holloway drew attention to this at the 1978 Catholic Renewal conference at Loughborough. As an illustration of the temptation to 'take a glory trip', Holloway cited the Betjeman poem:

> . . . under the Travers baroque, in a limewashed whiteness,
> The fiddle-back vestments a-glitter with morning rays,
> Our Lady's image, in multiple-candled brightness,
> The bells and banners – those were the waking days
> When faith was taught and fanned to a golden blaze.

But, he warned, defensive and negative movements which sought merely to recapture the past were not a sound basis for renewal.

> Negative movements, like negative theology, do not capture the hearts and minds of good men and women, only of the sick-minded, the marginal, the insecure. That could, but mustn't, happen to Catholic Renewal. We must not become

> a fanatical, self-righteous rump, a sort of ecclesiastical National Front.[26]

Since Loughborough there have been encouraging signs of a rebirth of a socially aware and healthy Catholicism, but the pathological aspects still give considerable cause for alarm.

Most importantly, there has been a loss of theological perspective within the Catholic movement. The 'regulative principle' of the Kingdom has been lost. Yet only when there is a dialectical relationship between the Kingdom of God and a society in turmoil can a genuine Catholic radicalism re-emerge.

3

Believing in the Incarnation and Its Consequences

The centrality of the flesh of Christ

'Regard the flesh, the body, matter, as evil or even inferior, and one has already begun the deviation from Christian truth.'[1] So writes the Indian thinker Paul Verghese in his study *The Freedom of Man*. Verghese argues that there are specifically five 'basic distortions', 'real deviations' in western Christianity: a low view of the incarnation of Christ, a flight from the world, a view of man as abject dependent, an emphasis on individual salvation, and a low view of the sacraments. They are very closely interrelated, but I want to draw attention specifically to the first as a central feature of a whole pathological syndrome. Verghese, looking at the West from the perspective of a Syrian Orthodox, over-estimates the malevolent role of Augustine whose 'incapacity to take the flesh of our Lord seriously' he stigmatizes.[2] But, he continues, 'this playing down of the Incarnation is at the root of many problems in contemporary theology including its overly eschatological orientation. Even the new theology of hope is based on a *promise* as in the Old Testament, not on the *fact* of the Incarnation which is the true starting point of the Christian faith.'[3] The undervaluing of the world and the low view of man are direct consequences of the low view of the Incarnation. Similarly, because there is a neglect of the body and of this world, salvation comes to be seen in a narrow individualistic way, and the sacraments, which depend upon a high view of the senses and of matter, lose their significance. Certainly in Augustine's thinking, the body has a low status. 'For not in the body but in the mind was man made in the image of God.'[4] I want to argue that the failure to take seriously the fleshly, materialistic basis of Christian faith is

B

crucial to many of our current problems in spirituality and in social action. For the Incarnation, the taking of manhood into God, is the basis both of Christian mysticism and of Christian social theology.

The Incarnation presupposes a high and optimistic (though not naive) view of man, for it was human nature which Christ assumed. Indeed 'the Christian understanding of God is wholly in terms of a human situation.'[5] But the West has suffered for many years from a low and pessimistic view of man, to such an extent that this has been taken as Christian orthodoxy. One sees this clearly in the popular writer of an earlier decade, C. S. Lewis. 'Unless Christianity is wholly false,' he wrote, 'the perception of ourselves which we have in moments of shame must be the only true one . . . Christ takes it for granted that men are bad. The real test of being in the presence of God is that you either forget about yourself or see yourself as a small dirty object.'[6] On such a view, a true Christian humanism is impossible. Contrast Lewis's description with the picture of man in the Vatican Council's document *Gaudium et Spes* (1965). Man, it says, is 'the centre and crown of all things'. 'He who follows after Christ the perfect man becomes himself more human.'[7] There is no denial of sinfulness, but a strong emphasis on man's glory, made as he is in the image of God. It is this view of man which I suggest is the orthodox Christian view, and I shall argue that orthodoxy of incarnational belief and a high view of man and of matter are intimately connected.

In the New Testament, the Incarnation of Christ is the basis of Christian mysticism. Through the flesh of Christ, we are brought into union with God: without the acknowledgement that Jesus Christ has come in the flesh, says St John, there can be no true Christian faith.[8] The idea of the 'body of Christ' is central to the theology of Paul. J. A. T. Robinson calls it 'the keystone of Pauline theology'. 'It is almost impossible to exaggerate the materialism and crudity of Paul's doctrine of the Church as literally now the resurrection body of Christ.'[9] So there is a true communion, a sharing in Christ's nature. We are sharers in the divine nature, St Peter says.[10] The divine seed (*sperma*) dwells in us, says St John.[11] The patristic writers take up the theme of sharing in Christ's divinity. Christ, said

Irenaeus, made the image of God secure 'by uniting manhood in the likeness of the unseen Father by means of the visible Word.' God 'became what we are that he might make us in the end what he is.'[12] There is a real participation (*metoche*) in God. It was this theme which Athanasius in the fourth century took up in his famous statement which can be literally translated from the Greek: 'he was humanized that we might be deified'.[13] The concept of deification (*theōsis*) has remained central to orthodox theology and spirituality. Man was created for deification, claimed St John of Damascus (675–749). But it all hinges on the Incarnation. As Athanasius says: 'Man could not be deified if joined to a creature, or unless the Son were true God. Nor could man be brought into the Father's presence unless it had been his natural and true Word who had put on the body.'[14] Much earlier, Tertullian had stressed how absolutely critical was the issue of the *flesh* of Christ. 'It is on the flesh that salvation hinges' (*Caro salutis est cardo*).[15] 'If Christ's being flesh is found to be a lie,' he continues, 'then everything that was done by it was done falsely . . . God's entire work is subverted.' In our own day, the Russian writer Paul Evdokimov has described the transfiguring of man through the Incarnation as 'Christification'. The formation of Christ in man, he says, is not an imitation of Christ, nor even the application to man of the merits of the Incarnation, but is 'the injection into man of the Incarnation itself'.[16]

In the orthodox tradition the Incarnation is the basis of the mystical life: only if the human Christ is divine can there be, through him, a true communion with God. 'God is an intimacy in the flesh that otherwise is death.'[17] But it is from the Incarnation too that the Christian social tradition derives. For if manhood has been taken into God, the human race is a solidarity, men are oned with God and with each other. 'You have seen your brother, you have seen your God', wrote Clement of Alexandria, quoting an alleged saying of Jesus. If manhood has been truly taken into God, then the gospel saying 'Inasmuch as you did it to the least of my brothers, you did it to me' becomes a terrible theological truth, and not merely figurative language. Christian social theology must stand by an assertion of the theological unity of the human race. 'Our total communion is expressed in living with the man thrown down upon all the highways of the world and wounded by every act of brigandage in history, in the unique outpouring of the blood of the Poor One.'[18] The recognition of the divine image in man and of the extension of the Incarnation into the world is crucial to a sound social and political theology. To put it another way, the roots of spirituality and of socio-political action are identical: the decay of one is coincident with the decay of the other, for both depend on a communion with God and with man through the Incarnation.

Today, part of the pathology of western Christian life is the destruction of the essential unity of the mystical and the socio-political, the contemplative and the prophetic. Mysticism and politics are seen at best as alternative modes of discipleship, at worst as incompatible and ideological opposites. So we have forms of escapist, pietistical, anti-incarnational spirituality on the one hand, and forms of fanatical, inhuman, anti-incarnational political movements on the other. In both one sees a failure to treat the human seriously. Certainly there is a good deal of spirituality about, and the identification of false forms of spirituality is a critical issue. For Christians, one of the earliest diagnostic tests of true spirituality is in the First Letter of St John: 'every spirit which does not confess that Jesus Christ has come in the flesh is not of God'.[19] This tradition was in sharp conflict with that of the Neo-Platonists which associated matter with the second-rate and the inferior, and it conflicts with our contemporary forms of pseudo-mysticism which seek escape from 'materialism' into a world of 'pure spirit'. For the Christian mystic, love of God and love of the brother/sister are inseparable. Spiritual gifts without charity are worthless. According to the fourteenth-century mystic Ruysbroeck, those who teach and practise the attainment of tranquillity as the goal of mysticism and disregard fraternal charity and ethics are guilty of spiritual wickedness: they are, he says, 'the most evil and most harmful men that live'. But today it is precisely this kind of non-social, non-prophetic, non-incarnational mysticism which we see so frequently, with its self-centred concern for the attainment of inner peace, its violent polarization between the spiritual and material world, and its inevitable trend towards elitism and away from common humanity. It is not only, or mainly, outside the

Christian tradition that we see such false spirituality. There is ample evidence that a good deal of the spirituality associated with the new Pentecostalism is of this type. The emphasis on love, joy, peace, warmth, and praise is not always accompanied by the contemplative struggle, conflict with the fallen world-order, the solidarity of mankind, or the preaching of the Kingdom. There is a breakdown which is ultimately theological: a failure to take seriously the Word made flesh, the redemption of the body and of matter.

If spirituality which cuts itself off from the political becomes escapist, social and political movements apart from spirituality become anti-human and ultimately totalitarian. Marcuse saw this, though he did not see its application to his own thinking. 'Unless socialism is built by such a new type of human being, the transition from capitalism to socialism would mean only replacing one form of domination by another form of domination.'[20] In other words, the new society is inseparable from the new man, politics and spirituality are inseparable. The mystic tends to forget the one, the revolutionary forgets the other. If the solidarity of humanity is forgotten, mysticism becomes a form of spiritual self-delusion. But if the sacred value of each person is forgotten, if contemplation is despised as a non-productive luxury, if spiritual progress is seen as manifested in the world but not in me, the result must be a disregard for people. The small man goes to the wall, he is dispensable. Ghandi realized this when he said, 'Recall the face of the poorest and most helpless man whom you have seen, and ask yourself if the step you contemplate is going to be of any use to him. Will he be able to gain anything by it? Will it restore him to control over his own life and destiny?'[21] The critical link between the small man and the collective, the link which the Incarnation stresses, is recognized also by the Latin American writer Paulo Freire:

> The oppressed who have been shaped by the death-affirming climate of oppression must find through their struggle the way to life-affirming humanization, and this does not lie simply in having more to eat (though it does involve and cannot fail to include having more to eat). The oppressed have been destroyed precisely because their situation has

> reduced them to things. In order to regain their humanity they must cease to be things and fight as men. This is a radical requirement. They cannot enter the struggle as objects in order *later* to become men.[22]

Contrast this with the approach of two popular writers in the mystical scene of this century, both of them with considerable followings. Alan Watts, at the climax of his revealing study *The Joyous Cosmology*, sees at last the opening up of his understanding of the cosmic order – 'dawning into a colossal clarity as if everything were opening up down to the roots of my being and of time and space themselves'. And what is this insight? 'The sense of the world becomes totally obvious . . . There is simply no problem of life: it is completely purposeless play – exuberance which is its own end . . . Pain and suffering are simply extreme forms of play, and there isn't anything in the whole universe to be afraid of because it doesn't happen to anyone.'[23] Or take the account by Teilhard de Chardin, now so fashionable in some liberal circles, of the role of suffering in human progress:

> The world seen by experience at our level is an immense groping, an immense search, an immense attack: its progress can take place only at the expense of many failures, of many wounds. Sufferers of whatever species are the expression of this stern but noble condition . . . simply paying for the final march and triumph of all. They are casualties fallen on the field of honour.[24]

It was Teilhard who hailed the dropping of the atomic bomb on Hiroshima as a sign of the hallowing of man![25] In both these writers there is a frightening disregard for human suffering, for the poor, the oppressed, the small man. In Watts it is all illusion, in Teilhard it is all necessary. In both, whether through a Gnostic anti-materialism, or through a kind of theological Stalinism, the poor man is dispensable.

The continuing significance of heresy

Now I want to suggest that the doctrine of the Incarnation is central to the recovery of a materialistic spirituality and a spiritual materialism: that is, a spirituality which treats the material order and its structures of injustice seriously (as

Watts did not), and a materialism which treats the Spirit in each person seriously (as Teihard did not). Deification cannot occur if you are dispensable, nor can human suffering be healed if it is illusory. I want, therefore, to argue that the debates about the nature and person of Christ were far from irrelevant doctrinaire arguments but were in fact of the most vital significance. 'The battles the believers of the faith fought against the heretics', wrote the nineteenth-century Anglican socialist Thomas Hancock, 'they fought not only for the church but for humanity.'[26] Moreover, the early heresies are by no means extinct: on the contrary, there has been a survival, and in recent years a powerful resurgence, of the major ones. Let me draw attention to four of the christological heresies which are evident in our day, all of which have major repercussions outside the strictly dogmatic area. The heresy of Eutyches is often misleadingly called the Monophysite heresy. Eutyches, who was deposed at the Council of Chalcedon in 451, held that there was only one nature in Christ, the divine. The practical consequence of this view is that there can be no redemption for the human situation, for the gulf between the divine and human is absolute. It has been said that Mr Enoch Powell's theology is Monophysite, for in his understanding of the God–world relationship, there seems to be no possibility of any real contact between the one and the other. The Kingdom of God remains wholly spiritual and wholly futuristic, as it did for Luther. So Powell says:

> I cannot as a politician assume that what will happen when the Kingdom comes is happening or has happened . . . I find it insuperably difficult to draw deductions from my Christian religion as to the choices which lie open to me in my political life . . . the essential teachings of Christianity . . . seem to me, characteristically and essentially, both to be absolute and to be in deliberate and direct conflict with human reality and human experience.[27]

The paradox which Catholic theology has sought to maintain is here recognized, but Powell resolves it, not by an incarnational theology (God the Absolute taking human reality and human experience into himself) but by a 'Monophysite' theology in which the two realms, divine and human, are totally separated. The consequences for Christian social and political thinking are obvious.

Another heretical revival has been that of Gnosticism. 'Gnosticism, ancient and modern, is basically the understanding of theology as self-awareness.'[28] Forty years ago, Jung claimed that 'the spiritual currents of the present have, in fact, a deep affinity with Gnosticism', and he pointed to the interest in psychic phenomena, spiritualism, occultism, astrology, and so on.[29] Historically, the Gnostics have exhibited three characteristics: first, a stress on secret knowledge – Origen in the third century spoke of 'certain secret principles' by which the soul enters the body – reserved for the initiates, and through which salvation, enlightenment, *gnosis*, comes;[30] secondly, a consequent division of the world into the initiates, the *illuminati*, those who are 'in the know', and the rest of mankind, the common herd; thirdly, the location of evil in *matter*. In all this, Gnostic spirituality is wholly and fundamentally opposed to incarnation. 'The Gnostic is self-centred'[31] – not God-centred. Gnosticism is elitist, anti-materialistic, and culturally conformist, and nothing could be more mistaken than the view, currently being propagated in its latest version, that the Gnostics were the original radical Christians. Today we see Gnostic features in many of the syncretistic eastern cults, meditation schools, occult sects, and in sections of the Christian world where the Word made flesh is reduced to the Word spoken in secret to a select company.

We also see a revival of the Marcionite heresy. Marcion, who died around 160, held that the Christian gospel was one of *love* alone, not wrath. 'All you need is love' was the Marcionite slogan. Consequently he repudiated the Old Testament as the book of God's wrath, despotic, violent, and cruel. The God of love, revealed in the gentle Jesus, was set against the God of wrath. Marcion, like the Gnostics, held a *docetic* view of Christ's humanity and sufferings: they were apparent and not real. The result was a naive, sentimental theology which failed to do justice to humanity or to the nature of evil. Its modern equivalent can be seen in the theological liberalism which removes from the liturgy everything that speaks of woe, wrath, and violence, especially noticeable in the Anglican Liturgical Commission's prostitution of the Psalter. But modern Marcionism is most marked in the sentimental love culture which Rollo May has called 'pseudo-innocence'.[32] The innocent person in religion who lacks the wisdom of serpents can do considerable damage both to himself and to others. Innocence is the enemy of spirituality, for true spirituality comes from a *deeper* awareness of and encounter with good and evil. 'Innocence that cannot include the daimonic becomes evil.'[33] The God of Marcion was so good, so gentle, so pure, so antiseptic, that he could not, and therefore did not, enter the filth and mess of human history and materiality.

The most destructive and most common of all the great heresies is Arianism. Arius, the fourth-century priest of Alexandria, held that the essence of God could not be shared or communicated. Therefore the Son of God was a creature, a demi-god. Arianism was condemned by the Council of Nicea in 325 but continued to flourish, and the Emperor Constantius made it the official imperial religion. Not until the Council of Constantinople in 381 was orthodoxy finally victorious. The conflict with Arianism was no mere theoretical debate, but raised all the central issues of Christianity. For in Arian theology, there can be no real relationship within the Godhead, between God and man, or between man and man. The Arian world is one of separation, the Arian God is characterized by his otherness. It was against this view that Athanasius stressed that 'man could not be deified if joined to a creature, or unless the Son were true God'.[34] But Athanasius also saw that Arianism was the theological glorification of imperial tyranny. The Arian god was like the Roman Emperor: sublime, remote, despotic. For sharing and communion disappear from the heart of the Godhead. God ceases to be a social God and becomes a tyrant. Athanasius saw a close connection between the theology of the Arians and their oppression of the poor. 'Human nature is prone to pity and sympathizes with the poor. But these men have lost even the common sentiments of humanity.'[35] Thomas Hancock in the nineteenth-century pointed to the relevance of the attack on Arianism:[36]

If there be no absolute co-eternal Son, there can be no

> absolute eternal Father. Unless there be an only begotten Son of God, unless this only begotten Son be the One in whom all consist, we may have an omnipotent Manufacturer – or rather some omnipotent Manufacturer may have us, as the potter has the vessels, but we men can have no Divine Father.

Against this view, Hancock argued that, if the facts set forth in the Athanasian creed are not true, then we are orphans, and there is no gospel. His colleague, Stewart Headlam, also saw the Incarnation as the foundation of his social thinking. Thus, in his defence of the stage and of ballet-dancing against the contemporary equivalents of the Festival of Light, he wrote, on 7 August 1881:[37]

> The Athanasian Creed teaches that the manhood has been taken into God; that it is necessary to eternal salvation that we believe rightly the Incarnation of our Lord Jesus Christ; that the Holy Spirit is incomprehensible, immense, boundless in his influence. These are the theological facts on which I base my vindication of the stage.

This was written against a background of a decadent Victorian Christianity whose god was Arian: remote, moralizing, despotic. That Arian god still rules in much of the distorted Christianity of the west. We may see formal Arianism in such groups as Jehovah's Witnesses where the Arian exegesis of Scripture is used, or in sections of the Jesus Movement where the vicious God the Father is set against the gentle loving Jesus. But Arianism is all around us. It is the conventional 'establishment' English view of God. 'The creed of the English', claimed Alasdair MacIntyre, 'is that there is no God, and that it is wise to pray to him from time to time.'[38] Or, as the writing on the wall put it, 'God isn't dead – he just doesn't want to get involved.' In other words, the Arian god. He cannot get involved, by his very nature. Arianism speaks of a cruel and cold universe, of a god with whom we can have no relationship except that of a slave to a tyrant, of a Jesus who has not raised manhood into God. The inevitable result of this theology, now as in the fourth century, is a Church conformed to the world. For the Incarnation is the basis of a true Christian radicalism: a disincarnate, other-worldly theology in practice leads to this-worldly conformism.

Materialism and spirituality

I have argued that the christological heresies are extremely relevant to our present situation, and that they have important social and spiritual consequences. I want finally to stress that the urgent need to which the Incarnation calls us is the rediscovery of theological *materialism*. The 'taking of manhood into God', as the Athanasian Creed expresses it, has three major consequences for Christian thinking. The first is that *all theology is mystical*. Theology is concerned with deification, with divine union, with Godmanship (to use one of Alan Watts's happier phrases). To see mysticism as a department of theology is mistaken, for all theology is mystical theology. The theology behind the Nicene Creed is mystical theology. There can be no orthodox Christian theology which is not mystical. Evagrius of Pontus saw this in the fourth century: 'A theologian is one whose prayer is true.'[39] The eastern tradition has always refused to separate theology from spirituality, and has rooted the mystical quest in the dogmas of Trinity and Incarnation. The mystery of God's being, which is so strong a theme in the eastern fathers, is reproduced in the mystery of man, for through the Incarnation, through sacrament and prayer, God and man are oned. And this unity is not mental but also sensual. It is expressed powerfully in the fourteenth-century English mystic Julian of Norwich:[40]

> For I saw with absolute certainty that our substance is in God, moreover that he is in our sensuality too. The moment the soul was made sensual, at that moment was it destined from all eternity to be the City of God. And he shall come to that City and never quit it . . . Our substance and sensuality together are rightly named our soul, because they are united by God. That wonderful city, the seat of our Lord Jesus, is the sensuality in which he is enclosed, just as the substance of our nature is enclosed in him, as with his blessed soul he sits at rest in the Godhead.

Union with God is therefore the heart of theology, and is rooted in Christ's taking of manhood into God. 'In the Incarnation and its "spiritual" extension in a community, man is built into God's self-disclosure.'[41]

All theology is materialistic. Or, rather, all orthodox Christian theology is materialistic, rooted in a high doctrine of the body and of matter, and contrasting sharply and fundamentally with all forms of Gnostic and anti-materialistic spiritual movements. The taking of human flesh by the Godhead is central to Christianity. In the Te Deum as we sing it in Anglican churches, we lose the physical crudity of the Latin: *Tu ad liberandum suscepturus hominem . . . not* 'When thou tookest upon thee to deliver man', *but* 'When thou tookest upon thee man, to deliver him'. It is on the flesh that salvation hinges. The glory of God, as Irenaeus says,[42] is a living man. Or, as St John of Damascus put it in the eighth century:[43]

> I do not worship matter, but I worship the Creator of matter who for my sake became material, and accepted to dwell in matter, who through matter effected my salvation. I will not cease from reverencing matter, for it was through matter that my salvation came to pass.

It was on the basis of this theology that St John defended the use of beauty and art in worship against the iconoclasts who rejected pictures because they rejected the full humanity of Christ. The rejection of art and beauty, of human passion and amusement, derives from a more fundamental rejection of, and mistrust of, the body. It is this which is fundamental to Gnosticism in every age, including our own.

Sam Keen, one of the founders of the Esalen Institute in California, has written of the danger of the Gnostic rejection of the flesh and of matter in his essay 'The importance of being carnal: notes for a visceral theology'. Neither the Christian nor the secular cultures in which he had been nurtured, Keen complains, have given him adequate categories to interpret the language of the body and the senses. In spite of some improvements in our time, Keen says, 'there remains a deep-seated suspicion of the carnal enthroned in the Christian understanding of history and salvation. Nothing less than a major theological revolution will allow Christianity to escape from the heresy of gnosticism.'[44] Keen goes on to stress the urgency of realizing the meaning of incarnation as a principle governing the God–man relationship in all human life. 'The Incarnation, if it is anything more than a "once upon a time" story means grace is carnal, healing comes through the flesh.'

The factor which governs full incarnation is the willingness to trust the body, to trust the solidarity of my flesh with all flesh. 'Reverence the flesh of all men as you reverence your own.' 'This imperative', says Keen, 'rests upon compassion, or dramatic identification with the flesh of another. It is this identification which is the basis of ethics.'[45] On the other hand, 'Gnosticism consistently saw an alien god (the Demiurge) as the creator of the body, the polis and the cosmos. Thus all were equally suspected and rejected by the man in quest of salvation.'[46] Refusal to accept the flesh and refusal to accept the world are closely connected, for both are seen as alien to God. It is not therefore accidental that campaigns against 'moral pollution' are often associated with right-wing political positions, for the alien forces must be opposed by tight controls and rigid laws. Paradoxically, and as a direct consequence, the true renunciation of both the flesh and the world – in the correct sense of the baptismal liturgy – is modified to the point of compromise with both.

The assertion of the sacredness of the flesh and of matter is of prime importance in the recovery of a Christian social theology. It involves taking very seriously the ethical issues in such areas as psychosurgery, abortion, physical psychiatry and the use of psychoactive drugs, aversion therapy, and nuclear energy. It is fundamental to the understanding of racism and of sexuality. It is the central question about teetotalism which often involves far more than a difference in personal life-style, revealing deep cleavages in doctrine. For if wine is incapable of sanctification, it is impossible that it can become the Precious Blood of Christ. Indeed the issue of the Real Presence of Christ in the Sacrament is closely connected with that of his Incarnation and his presence in matter. Historically the belief that matter is evil or inferior tends to lead to both false spirituality and an irresponsible approach to the material world. The flesh and matter are consigned to the regions of the sordid and the 'profane'. 'Do people never think when they read the writing on the lavatory wall? . . . It is the measure of our lostness that we relegate the direct statement of our origin (and in some cultures of our end as well – four letter words for death!) to the public convenience.'[47] So much of our religious life is based on denial of the sacredness of the flesh and of matter that orthodoxy is seen as outrageous.

All theology is social. There is no 'social gospel': the gospel is social. 'Social action' is not an implication. If Christ has raised manhood into God, it follows that there is a true sharing in the common life of the Godhead. God is not remote, a super-object, a person. It was this kind of idolatry which the dogma of the Trinity was aimed to counter. The issue is really vital, for it involves two incompatible views of God. The contemporary orthodox theologian Vladimir Lossky puts it well when he writes of the Trinity:[48]

> The Trinity is . . . the unshakeable foundation of all religious thought, of all piety, of all spiritual life, of all experience . . . If we reject the Trinity as the sole ground of all reality and of all thought, we are committed to a road that leads nowhere, we end in an aporia, in folly, in the disintegration of our being, in spiritual death. Between the Trinity and hell there lies no other choice.

4

Contemplation and Resistance as seen in the Spirituality of Thomas Merton

The search for spiritual roots

In a paragraph which has now become justly famous, Daniel Berrigan described the pursuit of contemplation as a strictly subversive activity, a political act implying the riskiest of consequences to those taking part.[1] The rediscovery of the necessary unity between contemplation and resistance, the mystical and the prophetic, is perhaps the central need of modern western Christianity. Berrigan saw the need in the United States for a powerful upsurge of spirituality which would redeem a decayed civilization. 'The American psyche', he wrote, 'cannot become the fraternal instrument of world change until it has undergone its dark night of the soul.'[2] Americans, he claimed, had become alienated from spiritual values by technology and the pursuit of power and wealth, and only a renewal of contemplation could heal that sickness.

Yet Berrigan was aware of the likely growth of false spiritualities. He warned that

> . . . in the derangement of our culture, we see that people move towards contemplation *in despair*, even though unrecognized. They meditate as a way of becoming neutral – to put a ground between them and the horror around them . . . We have a terrible kind of drug called contemplation.

Such contemplatives, he says, are cut off from social prophecy, and so 'they become another resource of the culture instead of a resource against the culture'.[3] A spiritual quest which is concerned only with the private world of the individual, with the attainment of his own 'enlightenment', can easily be absorbed by the culture. Capitalist society can make contemplation itself into a commodity.

To divide contemplation from prophecy is to damage and maybe destroy both. Berrigan's theme, that they are in fact a unity, is one which has been occurring in the work of many writers and thinkers in recent years. In an earlier age Charles Peguy wrote that everything worthwhile 'begins in mysticism and ends in politics'. Today from Latin America comes the call for a 'spirituality of liberation'.[4] From the young American pacifist writer Theodore Roszak comes the lament that the religious impulse has been exiled from our culture, but alongside it the view that 'it is the energy of religious renewal that will generate the next politics and perhaps the final radicalism of our society'.[5] From some young radical Christians in Britain comes a search for the 'spiritual dimensions to political struggle': 'the re-examination required was not so much a cerebral critique of theology or politics but a flesh and blood discovery of spiritual roots'.[6] It was with this search for spiritual roots that the monk Thomas Merton was concerned throughout his life.

The spiritual importance of Merton

Merton has been described by the leading American theologian David Tracy as 'perhaps the most significant Christian figure in twentieth century America',[7] while Dom Jean Leclerq has said that 'Merton was the man Christianity needed in a time of transition which began not with Vatican II but with World War II'.[8] His central significance lies in the fact that he embodied in himself the spiritual currents and crises of our age. In the person of this contemplative monk and prophet, several worlds met: the world of the renewed Latin church, of the rediscovery of eastern Christendom, of the non-violent movement, of the counter-culture, of Zen and the eastern mystical traditions, of political disenchantment and political revolt. Something of this integrative and unifying role was brought out in some words which Merton himself wrote in 1968:[9]

> If I can unite *in myself* the thought and the devotion of eastern and western Christendom, the Greek and the Latin

> Fathers, the Russians with the Spanish mystics, I can prepare in myself the reunion of divided Christians. From that secret and unspoken unity in myself can eventually come a visible and manifest unity of all Christians . . . We must contain all divided worlds in ourselves and transcend them in Christ.

In fact Merton's unifying role was far greater and wider than his own words suggest. Glenn Hinson, a Southern Baptist who knew Merton and studied his work closely, wrote in 1972:[10]

> Merton's originality lay . . . in the way he fed the whole tradition of contemplation through his own gifted and fertile mind and personality so as to create a profound new synthesis which could speak not only to his monastic confreres but even to the wider circle of humanity.

Merton's writings convey a profound experience of man's predicament in the modern world, and it was an experience which paradoxically he gained through monastic solitude. Like an earlier contemplative, Father Alfred Delp, a Jesuit who was in prison in Nazi Germany, Merton believed that solitude was a vital pre-requisite for the awakening of the social conscience. Delp had written:[11]

> Great issues affecting mankind have to be decided in the wilderness, in uninterrupted isolation and unbroken silence. They hold a meaning and a blessing, these great, silent, empty spaces that bring a man face to face with reality.

Merton wrote an essay on Delp's meditations which he saw as 'a penetrating diagnosis of a devastated, gutted, faithless society in which man is rapidly losing his humanity'.[12] Man's only hope was to recover his spiritual freedom and this involved recovering his ability to hear the voice in the wilderness. Delp had warned that that voice was becoming fainter and fainter and soon might not be heard at all. Merton commented:[13]

> Yet the 'wilderness' of man's spirit is not yet totally hostile to all spiritual life. On the contrary its silence is still a healing silence. He who tries to evade solitude and

> confrontation with the unknown God may eventually be destroyed in the meaningless chaotic atomized solitariness of mass society. But meanwhile it is still possible to face one's inner solitude and to recover mysterious sources of hope and strength.

Liberation always begins on the plot of earth on which one stands. 'In solitude, in the depths of a man's own aloneness, lie the resources for resistance to injustice.'[14] On the other hand, a resistance which has not been wrought out of inner struggle must remain superficial or degenerate into fanaticism.

Merton saw the 'spiritual life' as the life of the whole person. He rejected the smug self-assurance of the devout ones who know all the answers in advance, know all the clichés of the inner life, and can defend themselves against all the demands of being truly human. He knew only too well the dangers of 'bogus interiority',[15] the distortion by which self-study becomes merely the evasion of risk and struggle. Bogus contemplation, as evidenced in many of the fashionable – and profitable – meditation schools, was concerned to avoid conflict and reduce tension. But Merton emphasised the fact that 'Christian faith is a principle of questioning and struggle before it becomes a principle of certitude and peace . . . The Christian mind is a mind that risks intolerable purifications.'[16] The desert, as the place of struggle and purification, was a constant theme of his writings, and he once defined contemplation simply as 'the preference for the desert'.[17] For the desert experience was the experience of solitude in which God appeared to be absent. It was the presence of conflict and struggle which distinguished true silence from false. For true silence is 'a repeated bending over the abyss', whereas 'a silence from which he (God) does not seem to be absent dangerously threatens his continued presence.'[18]

Merton saw solitude and solidarity to be interconnected. The practice of solitude brings 'a deepening awareness that the world needs a struggle against alienation. True solitude is deeply aware of the world's needs. It does not hold the world at arm's length.'[19] 'The solitary, far from enclosing himself in poverty, becomes every man. He dwells in the solitude, the poverty, the indigence of every man.'[20] Indeed 'it is deep in solitude that I find the gentleness with which I can truly love my brothers.'[21] Solitude is thus necessary for the flowering of the common life of love and sharing. Thus he wrote of solitary prayer:[22]

> . . . the dimensions of prayer in solitude are those of man's ordinary anguish, his self-searching, his moments of nausea at his own vanity, falsity and capacity for betrayal. Far from establishing one in unassailable narcissistic security, the way of prayer brings us face to face with the sham and indignity of the false self that seeks to live for itself alone and to enjoy the 'consolation of prayer' for its own sake. This 'self' is pure illusion, and ultimately he who lives for and by such an illusion must end either in disgust or in madness.

In Merton's writings there are marked changes from the period of his early works, such as *Seven Storey Mountain* (1948) and *Seeds of Contemplation* (1949). The early Merton wrote from within, and for, the Roman Catholic community of the Counter-Reformation tradition. His assumptions were those of traditional Latin monasticism, and his audience came probably for the most part from within the Christian tradition. Merton himself stated that the author of *Seven Storey Mountain* was dead and that he had moved beyond that position. In fact, he called the Merton of that period a superficially pious, rather rigid and somewhat narrow-minded young monk.'[23] A fellow-Cistercian has described *Seven Storey Mountain* as 'pompous, arrogant, and judgmental',[24] while Daniel Berrigan observed that to judge Merton, as many have done, on the basis of that book would be like judging Aquinas by the graffiti on his playpen.[25] It was much later that the work of contemplation was consciously related to that of social criticism, and the crucial element in this was his philosophy of solitude. For it was in solitude that man became fully awake. It was this wakefulness, this insight and enlightenment, which preserved religion from fanaticism, and Merton saw fanaticism as the greatest temptation of the modern age. Merton's understanding of prayer is central to his social doctrine.[26] He defined prayer as 'a consciousness of our union with God',[27] and as 'an awareness of one's inner self'.[28] Self-knowledge, as all the mystics insist, is essential to sanctity, but it is only the beginning. We need to go beyond 'introversion', beyond the self, to God.[29] Prayer thus liberates us from self, and from all ideas of self. Merton held that the central concern with self led to the view of God as an object, and therefore eventually led to the 'death of God' ideas. There must be a real transformation of consciousness.

> This dynamic of emptying and of transcendence accurately defines the transformation of the Christian consciousness in Christ. It is a kenotic transformation, an emptying of all the contents of the ego-consciousness to become a void in which the light of God or the glory of God, the full radiation of the infinite reality of his being and love, are manifested.[30]

Spiritual progress involves the recognition of this false ego-consciousness, and Merton links this directly with individualism which has dominated western theology and politics for several hundred years. 'This individualism, primarily an economic concept, with a pseudospiritual and moral façade, is in fact mere irresponsibility.'[31] In confronting this false ego-consciousness, we begin the process of recovery of the divine image which is in all men.

What is crucial here is that behind this account of prayer is a view of salvation as a participation in God, *theosis*, a doctrine which is at the heart of eastern orthodox theology. Merton drew on the great theologians of the apophatic or negative tradition, and in particular on Gregory of Nyssa, in his understanding of man's sharing in the divine nature. 'God has made us not simply spectators of the power of God', wrote Gregory, 'but also participants in his very nature.'[32] Through the Incarnation, man is led into a mystical union which is not exceptional but is the normal Christian life. It is ironical that Merton died on the same day as Karl Barth (December 10th 1968) for whom such an idea would have been unthinkable. As a contemporary eastern writer has commented: 'A choice has to be made between early Barth or Basil and Gregory of Nyssa.'[33] Thomas Merton identified himself closely with the eastern tradition with its stress on the taking of manhood into God through the Incarnation, the basis of all Christian mysticism.

Monasticism and social criticism

It was against this background that Merton viewed the role of the monk. Monasticism was not to be seen as a subtle escape from the Incarnation and the common life of man, but as a specific way of sharing in the redemption of the world and of the common life. Monastic prayer is a deep confrontation with the alienation of modern man, and it is thus particularly vital to the undermining of illusion and falsehood. 'Merton understood that the unmasking of illusion belongs to the essence of the contemplative life.'[34] 'The monk,' he wrote in a paper given at Bangkok on the day of his death, 'is essentially someone who takes up a critical attitude towards the contemporary world and its structures'[35] He saw the future of the contemplative life to be closely linked with this critical role. 'The great problem for monasticism today is not survival but prophecy.' So others, including many non-Christians, have looked to Merton and to the monastic tradition for a new perspective on political struggle. Berrigan, for example, was steeped in the theology of Merton and learned much from him. Of particular importance in relation to Merton's influence on political activists was a retreat which he conducted in 1964 on 'the spiritual roots of protest'. Among the retreatants were Tom Cornell, Jim Forest, the Berrigans, A. J. Muste, and John Howard Yoder. John Howard Griffin commented on Merton's influence:[36]

> Many activists, those of us who were in the streets . . . understood and treasured Merton's vocation – it helped us to persevere when so many were dropping away. I have often said that we could not have done what we did without dedicated souls in monasteries to back us up. Merton was anchored in reality, and we looked to him to help us keep our balance and our sense of reality. Many of us . . . could vouch that, when desperate times came, when we seemed to be accomplishing nothing, when we were calumniated and threatened and tempted to give up, Father Louis and others like him salvaged us. We were not salvaged by the strategists or the sociologists but by men and women of highly advanced spiritual dimensions.

It is valuable to reflect on this impressive testimony when one hears the regular clichés about 'trendy '60s radicals'.

Merton's view of the role of the monk in the modern world comes out most clearly in his *Contemplative Prayer* and in his Bangkok paper on 'Marxism and Monastic Perspectives'. In the former work he argues that 'this is an age that, by its very nature as a time of crisis, of revolution, of struggle, calls for the special searching and questioning which are the work of the monk in his meditation and prayer . . . In reality the monk abandons the world only in order to listen more intently to the deepest and most neglected voices that proceed from its inner depths'.[37] The monk, he says, experiences in himself the emptiness, the lostness, of modern man, and he meets this at the point where the void seems to open out into black despair. But he rejects the way of despair, and through his prayer there comes healing. In his paper at Bangkok, he points out that the monk 'belongs to the world, but the world belongs to him insofar as he has dedicated himself totally to liberation from it in order to liberate it.'[38]

Merton thus saw the closest possible connection between the monastic vocation and the work of social protest. 'When speech is in danger of perishing or being perverted in the amplified noise of beasts,' he wrote in 1964, 'perhaps it becomes obligatory for a monk to try to speak.'[39] He described his own aim as being 'to keep alive the contemplative experience and to keep the way open for modern technological man to recover the integrity of his own inner depths.'[40] In 1968 he developed the theme of the monk as social critic.

> In speaking for monks, I am really speaking for a very strange kind of person, a marginal person, because the monk in the modern world is no longer just an established person with an established place in society. We realize very keenly in America today that the monk is essentially outside of all establishments.[41]

The monk, he went on, is a person 'who withdraws deliberately to the margin of society with a view to deepening fundamental human experience.'[42] Yet he also saw that the monk was a contradictory figure in the world, and that he 'cannot clearly explain himself to the rest of the world, and he is very foolish if he attempts to do so.'[43] Monks were essentially 'people who have consciously and deliberately adopted a way of life which is marginal with respect to the rest of society, implicitly critical of that society, seeking a certain distance from that society and a freedom from its domination and its imperatives, but nevertheless open to its needs and in dialogue with it.'[44] But it was a life which was 'in a certain sense scandalous'.[45] In 1957, writing on 'The Monk in the Changing World', he had concluded: 'In the night of our technological barbarism, monks must be as trees which exist silently in the dark and by their vital presence purify the air.'[46]

Thus the purification and liberation of man and the unmasking of illusion were to Merton essentially monastic tasks, and they drove him from contemplation to politics. Not in the sense that he modified his contemplative role, and began instead to campaign and demonstrate. Rather, his theological insight became political insight as an inevitable by-product. 'Christian social action is first of all action that discovers religion . . . in social programs for better wages, social security , etc. not at all to "win the worker for the church" but because God became man.'[47] The Incarnation was central to his social and spiritual teaching, and from the Incarnation he derived a fundamentally optimistic view of man. Like Gandhi whom he described 'he believed that in the hidden depths of our being, we are more truly non-violent than violent.'[48] For Merton, the crucial question in the debate over non-violence was whether evil was reversible. 'In the use of force, one simplifies the situation by assuming that the evil to be overcome is clear-cut, definite and irreversible. Hence there remains but one thing: to eliminate it.'[49]

Non-violence and the revolution within

Non-violence stands or falls on the view of evil. If evil is an irreversible tumour, then it must be cut out, and for this violence is necessary. Merton held that evil was reversible and could be changed into good by forgiveness and love. But 'only the man who has fully attained his own spiritual identity can live without the need to kill'.[50] So solitude and the inner quest are vital if peace on earth is to be attained. Yet non-violence is not simply a method of achieving a result. 'Non-violence is not for power but for truth. It is not pragmatic but prophetic. It is not aimed at immediate political results but at the manifestation of fundamental and crucially important truth.'[51] Merton, following Gandhi, held that non-violence is part of the law of human society, and that violence dislocates the social order. Violence is the law of the beast, non-violence the law of redeemed man. So the commitment to a non-violent life-style is a spiritual commitment, for only the non-violent in spirit can practise the non-violent life. Merton praised Gandhi for his recognition of the unity between the non-violent spirit and the struggle for human unity.

> This is his lesson and his legacy to the world. The evils we suffer cannot be eliminated by a violent attack in which one sector of humanity flies at another in destructive fury. Our evils are common and the solution of them can only be common. But we are not ready to undertake this common task because we are not ourselves. Consequently the first duty of every man is to return to his own "right mind" in order that society itself may be sane.[52]

The American pacifist writer James Douglass, whose thought owes a great deal to Merton, has described the essential unity of contemplation and action in terms of the Chinese symbolism of the Yin and the Yang. The earliest Chinese character for Yin was a cloud while that for Yang was a pennant or banner.[53] In his later years Merton found much guidance and illumination from the eastern spiritual teachers and especially from Zen.[54] His concern with Zen was no mere fringe interest. It was in Zen that he rediscovered the need to transcend the western divisions of matter and spirit, subject and object. In order to progress in God-consciousness, it is necessary to lay aside discursive reasoning and thought, and to go beyond the thinking process to the centre of Being itself. Merton, in a letter to William Johnston, the Jesuit priest who had found spiritual renewal through Zen, suggested that the apparent atheism of Zen was probably the rejection of the view of God as an object.[55] He linked the 'void' in Zen with the 'dark night of the soul' in St John of the Cross. In the darkness of contemplation, the idols and limited concepts of God are dissolved, faith is purified, and one is led to a deeper level of knowing in which the individual is transformed and made whole. He is liberated through darkness from idols within and without.

Thus the truly contemplative soul is a soul who sees clearly, sees too clearly for comfort. In his dialogue with the Buddhist Nhat Hanh, Dan Berrigan suggests that in a society where the machine seeks to control man's consciousness, contemplation must become a form of resistance. Merton held this view. 'A spirituality that preaches resignation under official brutalities, servile acquiescence in frustration and sterility, and total submission to organised injustice, is one which has lost interest in holiness and remains concerned only with spurious notions of "order".'[56] There is a spiritual basis for human oppression, and there are bogus spiritualities which cry 'Peace, peace' when there is no peace. The aim of Christian contemplation is not inner peace but the Kingdom of God, and this involves struggle and spiritual warfare. Just as the spiritual attack on Nazism came from men who were committed to a deep prayer and ascetical discipline, so Merton held that only the contemplative who had begun to see, through love, with the eyes of God, was able to provide the necessary resistance to evil which could not be deflected. Certainly his own path showed an ever-deepening perception and insight. James Douglass is one of many writers who testified to that:[57]

> It was early in 1965 and the war in Vietnam was coming home, though few really knew it. Merton knew it in his hermitage. He also knew that racism was stuck in the heart of America, when everyone else was singing 'We Shall Overcome'. Tom Merton prayed, listened, and wrote furious essays against the powers of destruction which he glimpsed first of all in himself. Merton seemed to know the way as no one else did.

5

Contemplation as a Subversive Activity

Spiritual renewal and prophetic protest

Increasingly the choice for Christians in the West is between established religion and biblical faith.[1] Established religion makes its peace with the prevailing socio-political order; it is a religion of appeasement, of accommodation and conformity, a religion from which struggle, conflict, and crisis have been removed. But once this has happened, the essentially prophetic stance of the Church is undermined. For prophecy and contemplative vision, of which prophecy is a by-product, depend upon the positioning of the Church at the overlap of the ages (cf. 1 Cor. 10.11). As Charles Péguy wrote: 'Everything depends upon that dovetailing of the temporal and the eternal. Everything collapses once that adjustment is unsettled, or out of true, or taken to pieces.'[2] The sun then goes down on the prophets; vision fades; the eyes close, or become glazed over.

Christian spirituality is rooted in the experience of the incarnation and passion of Christ. It is a Christ-ening, a putting on of Christ, so that our consciousness is changed. But this transforming process in Christ, this new creation, is distorted in established religion into conformity with the *status quo*. The troubled and troubling vision gives way to the cosy security of the glazed eye.

Prayer and contemplation, in established religion, become purely private practices within a social order which they neither question nor threaten. That order is simply a neutral backcloth for the practice of religion. Religion has become privatized, a phenomenon which some Christians actually welcome.[3] Not only that, the private religions have become a multi-million dollar industry. They are part of capitalism's success story – religions as commodities, religions which in no way threaten or disturb social stability. In this situation, the most urgent need for the Christian Church is for the recovery of the unity between contemplative vision and political struggle, the mystical and the prophetic, between the inner and the outer worlds. If the eye is sound, the whole body is full of light (Matt. 6.22), and the contemplatives are the eyes of the Church.

Now one of the central features of established religion is the removal of conflict and of spiritual warfare. For this religion is one of comfort, security, and safety. But the subversive character of Christian spirituality derives from the subversive character of Christ himself. The Christ of the New Testament was not a universally popular figure. He broke conventions, accepted the despised and rejected, and was condemned for political subversion. Simeon's prophecy that he would divide the hearts of many was a true one. He was a threat to the established order of his day, to the *status quo* in Church and state, to established religion. The Kingdom of God dislocated the stable order and it does so still.

The recovery of vision and the recovery of prophecy are indivisible, for prophecy is a by-product of vision. So it was with Amos and with 'the *word* . . . which he *saw*'. (Amos 1.1). It was out of his vision of the divine justice that he raged against the Bethel sanctuary and warned of a time of famine for the Word of the Lord (8.11). In 1967 R. D. Laing took up this prophecy of Amos and saw the spiritual famine and loss of vision to be an essential feature of our western society.[4] Five years later the same theme of loss of vision was taken up by Theodore Roszak. Our society, he argued, suffers from, indeed is based upon, a diminished mode of consciousness. The eye is no longer sound, and so our society has become a wasteland of the spirit, an idolatrous culture.

> Idolatry is not a moral failing: it is a mistaken ontology, grounded in a flawed consciousness . . . One need only ponder what people mean in our time when they counsel us to 'be realistic'. They mean, at every point, to forgo the claims of transcendence, to spurn the magic of imaginative wonder, to regard the world as *nothing* but what the hard facts and quantitative abstractions of scientific objectivity make it out to be . . . Religions are built at the boundaries

> of consciousness. We live in a world whose consciousness of reality ends at the scientific perimeter, hence a world growing more idolatrous by the hour.[5]

Idolatry is closely linked with loss of vision. In the Old Testament, the God of Israel is the living God who is known only within the process of life and obedience. The idols, on the other hand, can be known in themselves, for they are objects, and they are recognizable. They are the gods of established religion, from which the living God comes to set men free.

The Old Testament prophets moreover saw that idolatry is not simply a grave sin, but that it is the source from which other evils flow: and this is still true in our society. It is at this point that the terrible failure of established religion is exposed as a failure of *vision*. For established religion cannot *see*, and therefore cannot act, for action follows from vision. Contemplation therefore is concerned with clear perception, and this includes the perception of evil and oppression. The idolatry in our society leads to gross evils. To name only three: enforced poverty, the defacing of man, and sinful obedience. The enforcement of poverty through the unjust accumulation of wealth.[6] In western societies, the existence of gross inequalities of wealth and power, the concentration of economic power, and the growth of areas of poverty and deprivation, are not simply accidental and unfortunate blots on the urban landscape. They are inevitable elements in a society based upon organized injustice. They therefore constitute a spiritual problem for they are part of a false consciousness.

The defacing of man's image by reducing human beings to mere mechanisms. So the soul is vandalized and spiritual values are undermined.

The encouragement of wrongful obedience, one of the aspects of idolatry of which the early Church was most aware, and which was portrayed under the symbol of the worship of the Beast. Like pagan Rome, we too have become an increasingly authoritarian and repressive society, the society of the strong state in which the yes-men prosper. In such a society, the sane ones are those who are not plagued by doubt, those who obey orders without question.

Contemplation and conflict

The Christian pursuit of contemplation does not take place in space, but within this broken and fallen world-order. Contemplation has a context: it does not occur in a vacuum. Today's context is that of the multinational corporations, the arms race, the strong state, the economic crisis, urban decay, the growing racism, and human loneliness. It is within this highly deranged culture that the contemplative explores the wastes of his own being. It is in the midst of chaos and crisis that he pursues the vision of God and experiences the conflict which is at the core of the contemplative search. He becomes part of that conflict and begins to see into the heart of things. It is a painful experience, as Simone Weil saw:

> Man only escapes from the laws of this world in lightning flashes. Instants when everything stands still, instants of contemplation, of pure intuition, of mental void, of acceptance of the moral void. Whoever endures a moment of the void either receives the supernatural bread or falls. It is a terrible risk but one that must be run – even during the instant when hope fails.[7]

The contemplative shares in the passion of Christ which is both an identification with the pain of the world and also the despoiling of the principalities and powers of the fallen world-order.

We can begin to understand the meaning of the words of Daniel Berrigan:

> The time will shortly be upon us, if it is not already here, when the pursuit of contemplation becomes a strictly subversive activity . . . I am convinced that contemplation, including the common worship of the believing, is a political act of the highest value, implying the riskiest of consequences to those taking part.[8]

For the contemplative confronts the world of false consciousness and of systems rooted in false consciousness with the living Word of truth which pierces through the falsehood. It is an essential characteristic of contemplation that it unmasks illusion. Thomas Merton saw this unmasking of illusion to be the special work of the monk who must always assume a critical attitude to the world in which he is set. Through the monk's searching and questioning, his solitude and inner struggle, his exploration of the wastes of his own being, he listens more deeply to the hidden voices of the world.[9] So it is that solitude and communion with God lead to a greater and deeper awareness of the needs of humanity. This is true, not only of the monk, but of anyone who practises contemplative prayer.

Christian contemplation therefore is not a smug search for interior peace, for the resolution or reduction of conflicts and tensions. On the contrary, faith is a principle of struggle and purification before it becomes one of peace. The Christian mind is one that risks intolerable purifications.[10] The need for radical purification is expressed in the symbol of the desert, the symbol, above all, of contemplative prayer. The desert is the place of conflict in which God appears often to be absent or to assume terrifying forms. It is the place of spiritual resistance, of the encounter with evil, and of the purifying of our spirits. It is expressed too in St John of the Cross's symbol of the Dark Night through which all human souls in search of God must pass if they are to mature: a process of seeing by not seeing, of *agnōsia*, the way of ignorance.[11]

The solitude and inwardness which the symbols of the desert and the Dark Night express are essential to the common good, for without solitude, human society cannot become a communion but only a collection of separated individuals. It is in solitude, in the depths of man's aloneness, that there lie the resources for resistance to oppression. As Roszak says, 'We can now understand that the fate of the soul is the fate of the social order, that if the spirit within us withers, so too will all the world we build about us.'[12]

Thus Christian contemplation is rooted in the crudity and squalor, the despair and cosmic struggle, of the incarnation and passion. The vision of God is glimpsed within the world of matter. Contemplation is not a search for consolation or comfort or inner peace, however much these may at times follow. But, as Simone Weil wrote, 'love is not consolation; it is light', and she went on to point out that 'religion, insofar as it is a source of consolation, is a hindrance to true faith. In this sense, atheism is a purification.'[13] So much Christian preaching today makes Christ's teaching innocuous and tame by removing its central concern with spiritual blindness, truth, and wisdom, and concentrating exclusively on such areas as compassion, kindness, and sincerity. So Berrigan warned of a sort of pseudo-contemplation which is used as a drug, a way of shielding oneself from the horror and pain of reality.

False spirituality

Today, when there is a major resurgence of false spiritualities, it is worth noting that the dangers of pseudo-contemplation were familiar to, and condemned by, all the great mystics. *The Cloud of Unknowing* noted that 'the devil has his contemplatives'[14] while St John of the Cross warned of the harm done by an immature religiosity which acted as a positive impediment to spiritual growth.[15] One of the strongest attacks on bogus contemplation comes in the writings of the fourteenth century Flemish mystic John of Ruysbroeck. In *The Book of Supreme Truth* he wrote of 'the men who practise a false vacancy', who are 'turned in upon the bareness of their own being' but who mistake this state for God. They neglect the sacraments and the common life because they believe that they have 'passed beyond all these things' and have become super-spiritual. In fact, says Ruysbroeck, they are 'the most coarse and crude of all men living'.[16] In his *Adornment of the Spiritual Marriage* he returns to the same theme. What is the 'natural rest' which the false contemplative seeks?

> It is a sitting still, without either outward or inward acts, in vacancy, in order that rest may be found and may remain untroubled. But a rest which is practised in this way is unlawful, for it brings with it in men a blindness and ignorance, and a sinking down into themselves without activity. Such a rest is nought else than an idleness into which the man has fallen and in which he forgets himself and God and all things in all that has to do with activity. The rest is wholly contrary to the supernatural rest which one possesses in God . . .

These men are, he says, 'wholly attached, in their desire, to inward savours, and the spiritual refreshment of their nature. And this is called spiritual lust.' They 'believe themselves the holiest of all men living' but they are 'the most wicked and vile of all men living'.[17]

False contemplation does not only isolate the seeker in a spiritual cocoon, and removes him from the anguish and struggle of common humanity: it also dulls the consciousness and produces a spiritual blindness, an inability to see what is really happening. Whereas true contemplation awakens consciousness and heightens awareness, the false contemplation and false religion become, as Charles Kingsley saw, opium for the people. Kingsley was thinking of opium as a drug of escape from reality, whereas Marx, who later used a similar expression, used it quite differently, to refer to the analgesic (pain-killing) properties of the opiates. Religion might not be a way of escape, as Kingsley, Maurice, and most Christian Socialists had criticized it for being, but, so long as the causes of human suffering remain, religion may serve a useful role as a pain-killer.[18] Such an analgesic view of spirituality is far removed from a cross-centred spirituality and from true contemplation which heightens, rather than reduces, one's sensitivity to the pain of the world.

> Evil and good stand thick around
> In the fields of charity and sin
> Where we shall lead our harvest in.[19]

It is in the 'fields of charity and sin', of wheat and tares, of vision and compromise, the world of politics, in fact, that Christian contemplation takes place. The familiar picture of the Buddha sitting on the earth, with one hand pointing to the sky, and the other pointing to the earth, symbolizes our situation well. Vision and the daily round, must be held together if we are to avoid the false polarities of utopianism and reformism. Contemplative prayer is, at its best, a state of seeing, a deepening of vision, so that the will of God is more clearly seen, and the signs of the times more accurately discerned. It is this clarity of vision which makes Christian contemplation a truly subversive activity.

6

Spiritual Direction in the Present Climate

The contemporary context of spiritual direction

When I use the term 'spiritual' in this paper, I want to avoid any connotations of 'anti-material', or of seeming to refer to only one part of man, or to ideas of escapism. For the present, then, let us define spirituality in this way: it is the total, balanced, human progress towards a final glory. And let us see prayer as the key to that progress. Spirituality can in fact be seen as the whole art of living, of being human at its fullest, deepest level: and so spiritual direction is simply the application of the doctrine of prayer, and the practices, techniques, and methods which nurture it, to the needs of individual people. I want to suggest that the references we used to hear in the 1960s to 'secular man' and 'technological man' have proved curiously inapplicable to what has actually occurred. In many respects, we have entered a period of what Professor I. M. Lewis has termed 'an age of marginal mystical recrudescence'.[1] One can overstate this, but I believe it to be a fact that we are living in a time when the 'mystical dimension', contemplation, the search for spirituality, have revived, and much that was thought obsolete has suddenly surfaced again.

I want first to consider a number of facets of the background against which any spiritual direction must take place, and I can best do this by some personal testimony. Between 1967 and 1971 when I worked in Soho, I was conscious that there was a change in my work-pattern: a change from an emphasis on first-aid care, coping with drug overdoses, emergency homeless crises, and so on, to a specific concern with the needs of individuals seeking God. It is difficult to date this change precisely, but at some point around 1969 I became aware that, while we were not seeing any reduction in the numbers of people who came to St Anne's, Soho, for bread and cheese and for emergency help, we were seeing more people who wanted help about prayer, the meaning of life, the search for God. I found myself having to spend more time on really intensive work with individuals, most of whom were outside or just on the fringe of organized Christianity. So spiritual direction became an important facet of my ministry.[2]

Now I stress this fact because one of the standard questions which used to be put to me, with depressing regularity, at that time – usually by other priests – was 'Aren't you just a social worker in a dog-collar?' This was, in fact, precisely the opposite of what was happening. What seemed to be emerging was a demand for a priesthood which was concerned with guidance on the path to God. Now the peculiar feature of the Soho pattern was that most of the people who came my way for this purpose were not church people. So it seemed to me to be necessary to define direction in such a way as not to assume from the start an accepted body of doctrinal beliefs, or a clear ecclesiastical allegiance. This seemed to be a new factor in the situation which was not anticipated by most of the spiritual writers. What I needed was a model of spiritual direction which laid the emphasis on allowing the individual to find his own way, and therefore it was some encouragement when I found that this was not too far from the teaching of the old guides. So Father Augustine Baker wrote: 'The director is not to teach his own way, but to instruct his disciples how they may find the way proper to them.' The emphasis is on being a guide, in the current jargon an enabler, the emphasis is on seeking. In his book *Confession*, Max Thurian gives a definition of spiritual direction which seems to get the perspective right: 'Spiritual direction, or the cure of souls, is a seeking after the leading of the Holy Spirit in a given spiritual and psychological situation.'[3] So the director and the person being directed are both *seekers*. This is not a relationship of one person imparting enlightenment, wisdom, 'knowledge', to another person who is a wholly passive recipient. But it is a mutual exploration, a mutual seeking of the Holy Spirit. Many people dislike the term 'spiritual direction' because it suggests an authoritarian relationship, and I don't mind too much if we abandon it. But I can't think of a better term, and I prefer therefore to keep it and explain it.

There are three important backgrounds to the practice of spiritual direction today. The first is that of the spiritual quest which has been taking place outside the Church. We were finding in 1969 in Central London that many young people were identifying with such themes as the 'Age of Aquarius', the 'new consciousness', changes in consciousness, expansion, transcendence, whether through drugs or through non-chemical approaches. Sensitivity groups, encounter groups, meditation schools, chanting, were all in vogue. I have argued elsewhere that a good deal of this interest in new consciousness was anticipated in earlier thinkers such as C. G. Jung and W. B. Yeats.[4] In fact, most of the texts from the eastern spiritual traditions which have recently become popular in the counter-culture – texts such as *The Tibetan Book of the Dead* or *The Secret of the Golden Flower* – were originally introduced to the West by Jung. If one studies the works of Jung, one finds that they contain almost everything which has figured in the recent spiritual search and the rediscovery of the East. This new spiritual quest seems to me to have contained four facets: the chemical approach to spirituality through psychedelic drugs; the revival of eastern spiritual disciplines; the re-emergence of interest in the occult and paranormal; and the emergence of new forms of Christian expression such as the 'Jesus movements'.

I want particularly to draw attention to one characteristic of these varied movements: the desire for transcendence, leading to a concern with personal spiritual guidance, techniques, and methodology. What many people found in the eastern gurus and teachers, and did not seem to find in the clergy of the mainstream churches, was precise guidance about how to go about the business of praying and meditating. To put it in a cliché form, people seemed to want priests to be priests, and were complaining that it was difficult to get priests actually to talk about God! There seemed to be a sense that, if the clergy did not know about God, then it was best to go elsewhere to people who did. Many of the young people who had come through the drug culture and stumbled upon mysticism were surprised to find a book like *The Cloud of Unknowing* and to discover that there was a mystical tradition within orthodox

Christianity. They had assumed that mysticism was a non-Christian phenomenon. But they were even more surprised when they then found clergy who were totally ignorant of, or uninterested in, this tradition. Few clergy seemed concerned about the spiritual quest which was going on outside the Church, or concerned to offer it any guidance or direction.

A second background area is the discovery and development of the frontiers of theology and psychotherapy. In most of his writing, C. G. Jung was using categories which seemed to overlap with the categories of theological discourse. He was writing of the loss of the Spirit in the West, about the importance of powerful symbols through which one reached not only into the personal unconscious but also into the collective unconscious, and, perhaps, into some relationship with the Divine. He was writing of the importance of 'myth' at a time when many theologians were wanting to be rid of myths! Yet Jung was arguing that, if one loses contact with the world of myth, one ceases to be fully human. Jung was as concerned with the spiritual health of cultures as with the psychological health of individuals. For him religious consciousness was an integral part of psychological wholeness, With Freud, he saw the dangers of religion. But for Freud, religion was itself an obsessional neurosis, a disease. What Jung did was to turn the Freudian critique of religion on its head. There is indeed such a thing as unbalanced, pathological religion, but this occurs when religion becomes an escape from life. The true role of religion is to enable integration to occur, to enable the achievement of full humanity. So, because one can identify deranged forms of religion, neurotic forms of religion, forms of religion which have become distorted, warped, and harmful to men and women, this does not mean that all religion can be categorized in this way. There is religious pathology, but not all religion is pathological. For Jung, the distortion of religion was itself a pointer to the fact that it was an important part of one's being.

In recent years, R. D. Laing has exercised major influence, first, in his study of the origins of schizophrenia, and later in his explorations into transcendence.[5] Laing began to wonder whether the people whom we call 'mad' are not so much sick as on a journey. Maybe the mad see more than we do. Maybe those whom we call mad have somehow broken through, in a very painful way, to dimensions of reality which most of us have not seen. Laing's central point is that true sanity, as distinct from conventionality or 'normality', must involve breaking through the confines of the habitual ego, the ordinary waking consciousness. This ego is in fact only a small part of our total personality. If we remain at this level and never reach beyond it, we remain imprisoned within a very small part of ourselves. Laing was concerned therefore with transcending ordinary consciousness, with moving deeper into the unexplored regions of the psyche. So he and others within the field of psychotherapy have become more involved with exploring the world of spirituality.

Recently too we have seen the growth of what one must call 'casework theology', that is, the application of certain psychological insights and skills to pastoral care. There are many examples of this movement: Frank Lake's school of Clinical Theology, described in one enormous volume and many smaller ones, the skills developed by the Samaritans, the creation of such groups as the Westminster Pastoral Foundation, the recently formed Association of Pastoral Care and Counselling, and so on.[6] Frank Lake, in his early work, was essentially concerned with the identification of the schizoid condition, and he sees this, as does Rollo May on whose work he draws, as the fundamental disease of modern society.[7] Its main characteristic is the inability to establish close and deep relationships. Lake describes this disorientation of man, this splitting up of man into mind and body, as a very serious disturbance, and his concern is with trying to help people to rediscover wholeness, unity of personality, not to see themselves as minds which merely inhabit bodies. So there has grown up a whole industry of pastoral counselling and care which is concerned to learn from and utilize the insights of depth psychology about God and the relationship between God and human beings.

There are three points about this movement which need emphasis. Under the influence of sociologists, many social workers now regard the counsellor or caseworker as the enemy of social change, the person who papers over the cracks, making a fundamentally rotten system tolerable.

There is now in the area of social work a good deal of suspicion, in my view justified, of the kind of counselling which lays all the stress on personal disturbances and seems blind to the disorders within the social and political structures. So the interest in casework and counselling among clergy and among Christians generally has occurred at a time when, among social work students, there is an increasing trend away from casework and counselling towards a more committed political stance.[8]

The point also needs to be made strongly that what is often termed the 'dialogue between the Church and psychiatry' is a very uneven and unbalanced dialogue. It bears little relationship to most of psychiatry. The psychiatrists and therapists with whom theologians are wont to have 'dialogue' are not the vast majority of psychiatrists working in National Health Service hospitals, but a somewhat esoteric minority. Counselling, in spite of its spread and its value, remains for the most part a predominantly middle-class activity.

I believe that there has occurred what I can only describe as a retreat by some clergy into social casework and the therapeutic disciplines. The hostile critic who sees this retreat as a subtle exchange of one form of social control for another is not entirely unjustified. Of course, there are positive aspects to this development, for out of the insights of psychotherapy and social work has come a good deal of help for clergy in understanding the underlying mechanisms in spiritual direction. Spiritual direction cannot remain quite the same after psychotherapy. And yet the field needs to be subjected to some criticism, and I shall return to this later.

The third background to our present situation is actually the whole background of the Christian tradition of spiritual direction itself. In recent years some clergy have been very willing to learn from other disciplines, such as social casework, but have remained naively ignorant of the entire tradition of writing on spirituality which goes back to the early centuries of the Christian era. There is therefore a real danger that we lose grip on the spiritual tradition itself, and come to see ourselves in some kind of vacuum. 'Start from where you are', that most fashionable modern maxim, can easily be taken to mean 'Ignore the past', and it will tend in actual practice to mean 'Make the old mistakes again'. So let us look briefly at the Christian tradition of spiritual direction.

The spiritual director in the Christian tradition

The concept of a director, of a one-to-one relationship with a guide or spiritual father (*pneumatikos pater*) is a good deal older than Christianity. It appears in Buddhism, among the Sufis, in most eastern religious traditions, and outside religious traditions altogether. One finds it in some form in Pythagoras and in the Stoics. Within Christianity, one can locate the beginnings of one-to-one spiritual guidance in the Desert Fathers of the fourth century. Macarius, and later St John Climacus, became individuals to whom many went for help in prayer. The original spiritual directors probably were these desert contemplatives and hermits. In Russia, the figure of the *starets* survives to this day. He is the wise man to whom one goes for guidance on the health of the soul.[9] Our modern idea of spiritual direction in the West as an activity linked with the practice of confession goes back to the mendicant friars, the Franciscans and Dominicans of the late Middle Ages. It was from this time that direction became linked with the hearing of confessions, and this association has remained the norm in the western church almost to this day. However, the tradition suffered a severe narrowing in the period around and after the Council of Trent. This narrowing occurred specifically in three areas. First, the great directors of that period – St Ignatius Loyola, St Francis de Sales, and so on – were very concerned with the care of the 'over-pious' and the neurotic, and with what became known as the problem of 'scruples'. The scrupulous person was the person for whom religious devotion had become compulsive, and whose life had become an agonized search for rules and regulations. A good deal of spiritual direction was taken up with the problem of the over-pious and with unhealthy facets of religious devotion. Secondly, there was a stress in this period on the role of direction in fostering religious, that is, monastic, vocations. Thirdly, as one would expect, during this period spiritual direction was on the defensive. The defence of orthodoxy and the provision of 'safe' methods of prayer became central. So the tradition became a narrow one, and the confessional itself became over-involved with, and dominated by, canon law.

At the same time, one finds a very comprehensive view of spiritual guidance in the writings of St John of the Cross in the sixteenth century, especially in his two works *The Ascent of Mount Carmel* and *The Dark Night of the Soul* (which are in fact one book.) St John was concerned with the area of transition from meditation to contemplative prayer, and he was disturbed that many people seemed to 'get stuck' at a particular stage in spiritual growth, often because of bad direction. This was a worry also to St Teresa of Avila, St John's contemporary in the Carmelite Order. 'God preserve me from ignorant confessors', she prayed (though perhaps some confessors prayed that they might be preserved from St Teresa!). St John was very scathing about people whom he termed 'spiritual blacksmiths' who were responsible for hindering a person's progress by keeping him or her at a level of prayer which had in fact been outgrown. The whole emphasis throughout St John's writing is on the spiritual director's role in assuring the individual that what is happening to him or her is happening by divine grace, and that the point of progress in prayer is to become more and more open to the leading of the Spirit, allowing the prayer life to grow and flourish, and not to get stuck at one level. St John was equally concerned with the unifying of human life, with overcoming the conflict, which is so apparent in the early stages of prayer, between 'spirituality' and 'real life': and he saw the path through 'the dark night of the soul' as resulting not only in a greater awareness of God, but also in a deeper humanizing of the person who prays, an integration of heart and mind, Christian maturity.

I have written at length elsewhere about other spiritual guides.[10] For example, Père Grou, the eighteenth-century Jesuit, whose *Manual for Interior Souls* summarizes the aim of direction in a way which is very close to the descriptions of modern pastoral counselling. But at some point after the early eighteenth century, both in Roman and Anglican traditions, the concept of direction fell into decay. Dr Trueman Dicken writes of 'the authentic tones of a spiritual theology which had been silenced with the death of Jean Grou and were first heard again only in the writings of the Abbé Saudreau',[11] that is in the early twentieth century. There is certainly no doubt that spiritual direction went through a bad period. What was happening within English Nonconformity was that the concept of one-to-one direction was being replaced by preaching. In the writings of Wesley, there is only one reference to the cure of souls, and this is a reference to preaching. Within the Wesleyan movement, preaching to a great extent *was* the cure of souls, for it was in the long sermon that spiritual direction was given. The other important feature which grew out of Wesley's work, and which was strongly brought out in the Holiness movements which were inspired by him and which gave birth to modern Pentecostalism, was the stress on holiness, perfection, entire sanctification. In many respects, this concern with personal holiness was close to the idea of direction. Wesley was insistent that there were two stages in the Christian life. There was conversion and regeneration: but then there was also the 'Second Blessing', which some of his later followers called the 'Baptism of the Holy Spirit' (though they did not relate it to speaking in tongues but rather to holiness, purity of heart, and reception of the fullness of the Spirit's power). This stress on sanctification and ever-deepening holiness of life was a very central element in Nonconformity after Wesley, and we are only beginning to recover it today.

But in the liberal wing of Protestantism, one saw an almost total disappearance of spiritual direction. Liberal Protestantism was excessively rational, and was therefore not much concerned with the unconscious. It tended to be naively optimistic in its concept of social reform. It tended to stress – as it still does – leadership and 'impact', and it worked with a model of pastoral care based on the efficient use of manpower and resources. None of its emphases was particularly conducive to a concern with spiritual direction or indeed with close personal relationships. One American liberal writer, describing the fate of pastoral care within the liberal tradition, says:

> Metaphorically speaking, the first liberal (so far as the distance goes at any rate) might well have been the man who helped Jesus carry the cross to the place where he was crucified. With a job to be done, he was there. With energy to be spent, he had it. And in carrying a heavy cross, he was

> not drawn too close together with Jesus. Once the spot had been reached and the outcome was certain, he dropped from sight: we hear no more of this early liberal in the New Testament. Perhaps he was off to the Circuit Court, hoping against hope to get a reversal of the conviction, and having the courage to try. Or he may have been investigating the future support of Jesus' family or the burial arrangements, or he may even have been getting up a petition to Rome about Pilate. What he was about was no doubt of great potential significance. But at the place of crucifixion, he was absent once the cross had been delivered. For a liberal, the optimal social distance.[12]

I believe that this refers to something of abiding importance: the fact that a stress on manpower, efficiency, and management has often led in practice to a neglect of the deep things of the Spirit.

Spiritual direction and pastoral counselling

Within Anglicanism, there was a recognizable school of spiritual directors in the 1920s and 1930s, associated with such names as F. P. Harton (author of *The Elements of the Spiritual Life*), Hubert Box, F. G. Belton (who wrote *A Manual for Confessors*), Reginald Somerset Ward (author of *The Way*), and Evelyn Underhill. Martin Thornton has claimed that they represent 'a dying theological outlook' and are now 'obsolete'.[13] If anything has replaced this kind of school, it is probably the pastoral counselling/casework theology tradition associated with such names as Frank Lake, Michael Hare Duke, and the late Bill Kyle. And if there is anything corresponding to the older tradition of directors, it is perhaps to be found in the large number of clergy who have undergone Clinical Theology seminars and counselling programmes of various kinds. Is this satisfactory?

It seems to me to be important here to recognize certain key differences and certain dangers. The spiritual director is fundamentally concerned with God. The pastoral counsellor may refer almost exclusively to such concepts as 'human wholeness' and not necessarily to God at all. The director is part of a great tradition and he only has a purpose in so far as he is a part of the Body of Christ. The pastoral counsellor is less dependent on a tradition, he may be office-based rather than based within a sacramental community. More important, the spiritual director is not essentially problem-orientated. The pastoral counsellor is likely to be concerned a good deal with the emotionally disturbed, the deeply troubled, the damaged, the broken. It was once said that the caseworker judges success by the fact that people stop coming, but the priest judges his success by the fact that they keep coming! That is over-simplified, but it brings out the truth that the spiritual director's role does not cease when problems go away. He is not there to look for, or deal with, problems. His concern is wider. Pastoral counselling, on the other hand, particularly in the United States, has concentrated very much on emotional problems and difficulties. Again, the spiritual director is not concerned with helping people to conform socially. That may be a by-product in some societies, but it may lead in the opposite direction in others. Pastoral counselling has tended to encourage conformity, an aspect of it to which Thomas Merton drew attention.

Thus, while direction and counselling have close affinities, and while the traditions can learn much from each other, there are important differences. As a general rule, it is true to say that the spiritual director is presupposing health rather than sickness. Of course, there are similarities: the stress on mutuality, honesty, openness, non-directive work, sharing in a search, and so on. There is the very strong emphasis in both traditions on the fact that the director/counsellor learns as much from the person he/she is trying to help. Yet there is danger that if one puts all one's eggs into the counselling basket, other important dimensions are lost. The late Robert Lambourne, priest and physician, who until his death was Head of the Department of Pastoral Studies at Birmingham, wrote in 1970 of the limitations of a model of pastoral care which was based on pastoral counselling and casework.

> My thesis . . . is that the pastoral counselling called for in this country during the next twenty years cannot be built around a practice and conceptual framework derived from professional problem solving and prevention of breakdown.

> That practice and conceptual framework is based upon the clinical, medical and psychoanalytical models of the USA of twenty years ago, and it has proved inadequate . . .
> I believe that the pastoral counselling movement, most highly developed in the USA, must be seen as part of a too general assumption by society, epitomized by the medical profession, that we come to the good life by delineating problems and then either avoiding them (prevention) or solving them. Pastoral theology has been over-influenced by the puzzle-solving view of human progress – a 'hang up' theology which fits only too closely with the medical clinical professional identity.[14]

Lambourne's stress throughout his work was on the fact that pastoral care must be located within the Christian community, and that one is in danger of both theological and social distortion if it is based on a clinical model in isolation.

A relevant criticism comes from an American liberal writer, Daniel Day Williams. Echoing Merton's fear that pastoral counselling might encourage conformity and discourage social criticism, and Richard Niebuhr's view that the stress on counselling in the seminaries has led to the neglect of social ethics, Williams comments:

> The Christian ideal of life envisions something higher than freedom from anguish or invulnerability to its ravages. Its goal cannot be the perfectly adjusted self. In the world as it is, a caring love cannot but regard such a goal as intolerably self-centred. What does it mean to be completely adjusted and at peace in a world as riddled with injustice, with the cries of the hungry, with the great unsolved questions of human living as this? We see why in the end we cannot identify therapy for specific ills with salvation for the human spirit. To live in love means to accept the risks of life and its threats to 'peace of mind'. Certainly the Christian ministry to persons is concerned to relieve physical ills, anxieties, inner conflicts. But this relief of private burdens is to set the person free to assume more important and universal ones.[15]

One could set that comment alongside Daniel Berrigan's warning that, in a deranged culture, people may seek contemplation as a means of becoming neutral, as a resource of the culture instead of a resource against the culture. What Williams says about the search for peace of mind as an end in itself can be applied to many of the schools of meditation and 'spiritual development' which flourish today.

Some practical needs and problems

I want therefore to argue that we need a revival of spiritual direction which is non-clinical, which is not problem-centred, but which is rooted in the common life of the Body of Christ. This must involve also the emphasis on prophecy, vision, and spirituality in action. For we need to remember that the Christian life is a principle of struggle before it becomes one of peace. We cannot short-circuit the darkness and the conflict.

Finally, some points and questions about the practicalities of spiritual direction today. How can this dimension be got across at the level of theological training and post-ordination studies? It does seem to me that much of what is taught as 'theology' in colleges in a fairly remote, detached way is not what the great spiritual writers would have thought of as theology. To the eastern spiritual teachers in particular, there can be no theology without prayer, contemplation, and holiness of life. 'A theologian is one whose prayer is true' (Evagrius of Pontus). The priests of the future Church will be of little use if they are not closely in touch with this great tradition of living theology, a tradition in which the theologian himself must be changed and renewed. So we need more stress on the theology as the way of union with God. We need more stress on prayer as central, not merely an aid to doing some other job better, and for this we need more spiritual guides, and more time allotted to this ministry. How can we best use the resources of the religious communities, of the contemplatives, in this area? Do we perhaps need a new concept of 'oblature' which is geared to this age, to the needs of young people, of married couples, of communities living in the world? Again, how does one help today's 'over-pious', the people for whom religion of the unhealthy type prevents growth and maturity, and who raise as many problems now as in the days of St John of the Cross?

We need to extend and develop the dialogue between the Christian mystical tradition and the spiritual search which is going on outside the churches. In many cases that search may prove a very fruitful field for spiritual direction, but that will mean some reassessment of the role of the director in relation to the non-Christian seeker.

There is the question of spiritual direction within the movement of charismatic renewal. The charismatic movement desperately needs a St John of the Cross who can guide it beyond the experience of tongues and of the beginnings of infused contemplation which that experience may bring for many people. There are real dangers in this movement of elitism, of spiritual snobbery, of seeing tongues as a 'spiritual high', of sentimental obscuring of reality behind the seductive mystifications of charismatic jargon and ritual. Yet clearly the charismatic movement can bring new insights and help to renew the tradition, and this is evident in the renewal of sacramental confession itself. Compare the language of the Council of Trent's Decree on Penance, the language of the judge and the tribunal, with that of the Dutch Catechism where forgiveness is said not to be judicial but 'truly redemptive, deliverance, renewal, new creation'. The Roman Liturgical Commission of 1968 stressed the healing power of the sacrament, and this is brought out in the new rite of penance with its restoration of the stretching out of hands over the penitent. Here is true charismatic renewal of the sacrament, a sacrament now rightly seen as involving healing, strengthening, and guidance towards spiritual maturity.

If spiritual direction is as important as I have suggested, we need to assess our priorities in pastoral care and work. In Sunderland, a study of 33 clergy in 1970 showed that their average weekly work totalled 62.5 hours, of which 27 per cent was spent on 'pastoral care'. But only an average of 2 hours 40 minutes of the total consisted of 'personal consultations'.[16] What do we make of this in the light of the centrality of the one-to-one relationship and its place in the spiritual tradition?

We need to maintain the unity of spirituality and prophecy. The loss of the centrality of adoration must lead in the end to the absorption of the Church into the value-system of Mammon. Without the centrality of contemplative prayer and its vision of the Kingdom and the Glory, religion must degenerate into an opiate.

7
Spirituality, Psychotherapy and Politics

Psyche and spirit

In his study *Unfinished Animal*, Theodore Roszak writes about the future of psychotherapy, and while he writes from California, where things tend to look somewhat different, his words are a valuable starting point for this discussion:

> Our future image of human being, then, will be a strange, tense blending of the optimistic and the tragic: a study in paradox. We are optimistic in that we assume, not a radically 'fallen' human condition, but a whole and healthy nature at the core of us; not an original sin, but an original splendor which aspires to transcendence and succeeds often enough to sustain a godlike image of human being. We are tragic in that we see how easily, in our chameleonlike freedom, we misdirect that energy towards lesser goals, unworthy objects. The psychotherapy of the future will not find the secret of the Soul's distress in the futile and tormenting clash of instinctual drives, but in the *tension between potentiality and actuality*. It will see that, as evolution's unfinished animal, our task is *to become what we are*; but our neurotic burden is that we do not, except for a gifted few among us, know what we are. What is most significantly and pathologically unconscious in us is the knowledge of our potential godlikeness.[1]

Throughout the book, Roszak argues that one of the most important needs of the present is the rediscovery of the spiritual wisdom of the past. He ends the passage quoted above with these words:

> As all spiritual disciplines recognize, the will to transcendence may often concentrate itself in the 'dark night of the

> soul'. Disease means psychic tension and psychic tension is the potential energy of the spirit.[2]

There is a lot more in what he is saying, but I quote this passage primarily to illustrate the point that historically, and in actual practice, the border lines between psychotherapy and spirituality are often very blurred, and this seems to have been true for many centuries. Pastoral care and the healing of sickness in some form have been closely associated since the earliest times. So Sir James Frazer in *The Golden Bough* said that 'magicians and medicine men were the oldest professional classes in the evolution of human society.'

Psychotherapy and its critique of religion

In a recent paper,[3] the psychotherapist Irene Bloomfield looks at some of the areas where therapy and religion might conflict, and she makes three main points. She claims that religion tends to start with an ideal; therapy, by contrast, starts with the individual where he or she is. Religion may aim at holiness, but therapy aims at wholeness, involving the acceptance of our 'dark side'. She suggests that religion tends to neglect the unconscious, focusing too much on freedom and conscious choices. In fact, however, many people *cannot* love: we cannot feel the love of God if we have not felt the love of a human being. She argues that religion very often does not encourage honesty, stresses the 'ought' rather than the 'is', and fosters repression. It is essential that we accept thoughts in areas such as sexuality or anger, and accept that the thoughts are not as bad as the acts. In making these points, she has in fact identified some conflicts which range over a wider area than the specific conflict (if such it is) between religion and psychotherapy. If we were to pursue these wider implications, we should get into deep waters – for example, the conflict between idealism and realism which might well lead us into the Marxist critique of religion; the conflict between free will and determinism, with shades of Calvin in the background; and the conflict between repression and honesty with which a good deal of the contemporary western world is preoccupied. I want to suggest that these conflicts are not simply conflicts *between* religion and psychotherapy, but *within* religion itself, and perhaps within therapy.

It seems to be quite clearly true that *much* religion interprets holiness – I would say misinterprets it – as a rejection of the natural man and of the shadow. The question is whether this is true of *all* religion. 'Holiness is wholeness' seems to me to be a recurring theme in recent religious writing, almost to the extent of having become a cliché. We hear very frequently in Christian teaching about human potential, maturity, and growth, and in fact the association of holiness with maturity has its roots in the New Testament. The word 'perfect' (*teleios*) in Philippians is translated in the New English and Revised Standard Bibles as maturity, the emphasis being on movement towards fullness of life. J. B. Phillips translates it as 'adulthood'. The New Testament also includes a stress on what Henri Nouwen has called the wounded healer, the slain lamb, the stricken shepherd. Yet too often in actual practice religion creates its own artificial world, a world which preserves immaturity. St John of the Cross distinguished between religiosity and spirituality, arguing that there are forms of spiritual guidance which actually maintain people in their immaturities and prevent spiritual growth: he is probably harder on incompetent spiritual guides than any other writer since his day.

I accept all this as a criticism of some religion. Yet it seems to me that psychotherapy can also become a kind of religion, can create its own artificial world – the world of 'hang-ups' and problems. It is all too easy for people involved in counselling and therapy only to be happy when they are confronted with problem situations.

It seems to be true that much religion naively asserts 'free will', although it seems from recent press reports that this danger is more common among politicians – so Sir Keith Joseph on crime as pure free will – and among lawyers and judges than it is among clergymen. If anything, clergy today are inclined to make too many allowances for human frailty, and to understress responsibility. But historically there has always been a dimension in Christian theology which emphasizes the importance of 'principalities and powers' as the embodiment of evil, not simply within individuals but in social and political structures. The real emphasis behind the demonic symbol in Christian spirituality is the theme that there is evil embodied in structures which are not simply within the individual. I accept that there is some danger in Christian theology of over-emphasizing freedom: but there is also the opposite danger in some strands of theology – the danger of too much determinism. On the other hand, it would appear that psychotherapy and psychiatry are not exactly free of these dangers. We may forget that much of what is called psychiatry in the National Health Service is closely allied with chemotherapy, and that a good deal of chemotherapy is based on a highly mechanistic view of man.

I agree wholeheartedly that a good deal of religion does not encourage honesty. But the great masters of spirituality in Christian and other traditions constantly warn against the distortion of the spiritual life, stressing the importance of truth, insight, and clarity of perception as essential by-products of contemplative prayer. Of course, a good deal of religion can protect us from the truth, and there can be bogus forms of contemplation. As *The Cloud of Unknowing* says, 'the Devil also has his contemplatives'. Such false contemplation operates as a shield to protect us from reality, or as a drug to pacify us.

Yet again this does not seem peculiar to religion, and I suspect that the counselling movement can become a façade and a way of evading one's own problems. David Brandon puts this well:

> One neglected area, even by Illich, is the extent to which we hinder ourselves. Are there ways in which our practice of helping is used to stunt our growth as persons? Giving to clients can be a very effective way of concealing our deep-felt hollowness. I have frequently heard myself giving advice, guidance and love to people which I was completely unable to give myself. Helping and caring for others can be a very effective way of concealing desperate personal needs. It can conceal a need to control and even punish others. We may seek to be 'adequate in the face of the inadequacy of others'. Throughout most of my professional career I felt a continuing sense of fraud, of not being worth while, whilst trying to communicate the opposite to my clients.[4]

It would seem that Irene Bloomfield has correctly identified what we can call pathological manifestations of religion, rather than saying with Freud that all religion is intrinsically pathological. If this is truc, then it brings in the essential need for what the great spiritual tradition calls *diakrisis* (discernment) which is one of the central marks of spiritual directors from the Desert Fathers through to the great Carmelites of the sixteenth century, and is even more strongly emphasized in the eastern Orthodox tradition. Discernment and discrimination of the healthy from the pathological, discernment of sane religion from dotty religion, discernment of true spirituality from false: these are essential characteristics of spiritual direction. In fact, in the spirituality of the fourth- and fifth-century Desert Fathers, where the idea of the spiritual director developed within Christianity, we find many close similarities with the modern pastoral counselling movement. A very strong emphasis, for instance, on silence, on example, and on what, if the Desert Fathers were living in the twentiethcentury, they would presumably call the 'non-directive method'. A strong emphasis too on comradeship and togetherness rather than leadership and paternalism, and on helping the individual attain spiritual freedom.[5]

The contribution of Christian spirituality

I want therefore to consider the ways in which the tradition of spiritual direction within Christianity might throw some illumination upon the present dialogue between religion and psychotherapy. First, the spiritual director, in the mainstream Christian tradition, roots his or her ministry in the 'materiality' of incarnation, cross, and Kingdom. He is not idealist but realist. Against this, however, there is the constant danger throughout Christian history of Gnosticism. Gnosticism locates the source of evil in matter and the flesh. So spirituality comes to be a rejection of the flesh, a rejection of carnality, a rejection of nature. It is interesting that not only do the Gnostics locate the source of evil in matter and specifically in sexuality – and therefore some Gnostic groups become extinct on their principles! – but they also cut themselves off from the sacraments, believing themselves to be spiritually superior to the common material sacramental world. Further, they cut themselves off from the common life of the Christian community. So what we find is a spiritual elitism. And this does not seem to be peculiar to religion, and I suspect that there may be therapeutic élites too. So there is a need to affirm the material as the source of theology: we know nothing of God, according to the New Testament, except through the human and the physical. 'No one has seen God at any time; the only-begotten Son . . . has made him known' (John 1.18).

Now this can be accepted at a *head* level, but we need to accept it at a *gut* level, and to accept what Sam Keen has called 'the carnality of grace'. Christian theology again is inseparable from the passion, and this also has to be accepted at a gut level. There is no growth in the knowledge of God except through the experience of transformation and suffering.

Christian theology looks towards the coming of a kingdom of justice, love, and peace. There is always a danger in Christianity of 'super-spirituality' which seeks to attain peace, tranquillity, and spiritual achievement by bypassing the world of common humanity. But, again, is this a danger simply for the Christian? Robert Lambourne spoke in one of his papers of 'the fear of flesh and politics', a fear which he attributed to existentialism. He wrote:

> Sometimes one feels that the particular fleshy historical body of Jesus Christ is an embarrassment to Rudolph Bultmann, and that the particular abnormal cell structured brain is a defilement to which R. D. Laing cannot admit. Both psychotherapy and theology seem tempted to seek a docetic saviour.[6]

An important theme of the spiritual tradition at its best has been the close association between the knowledge of self and the knowledge of God. Of course the early Christian fathers did not use the language of the unconscious, but it is difficult to read Gregory of Nyssa without feeling that he at least knew what it was about. In his writings of the fourth-century, we find the view that to hold that man is made in the image of God means that man is a mystery because the Holy Trinity is a mystery; and to be made in the image of God is to share in the mystery of God's being. He deduces from this the conviction that there are hidden depths within the human personality. Now spiritual direction has been concerned with these hidden depths, concerned with self-knowledge and self-transcendence. In the 1960s Bishop John Robinson discovered the concept of God as 'the ground of being' and thought that Paul Tillich had invented it! In fact it was very evident in much medieval mysticism. The theme of God as the 'spark of the soul', as the deepest, innermost ground of human personality, is a very common theme, particularly in Ruysbroeck and in Julian of Norwich (who says that God is closer to us than we are to ourselves, and therefore it is easier to know God than to know oneself). The theme that you descend deeper into yourself in order to know God was taken for granted by most of the medieval mystical writers. The theme of the 'dark night' or, as in Zen, 'the void', is very much concerned with the transformation of human consciousness. This is something which we need to look at far more deeply: for sometimes religion seems to preserve us at a particular level of consciousness rather than aid this transformation.

A factor in spiritual direction is that, at its best, it has been concerned with conflict and crisis rather than with evasion. The Desert Fathers were most emphatic that, whatever else the spiritual guide should be, he must be a man of experience. So St Isaac the Syrian in the sixth-century says: 'Confide your thoughts to a man who, though he lack learning, has studied the work in practice'; and St Simeon in the eleventh century says: 'Seek an experienced teacher with knowledge of the passions'. The expression 'knowledge of the passions' comes up over and over again in the characteristics of a good spiritual guide. St. John of the Cross, in *The Ascent of Mount Carmel* and *The Living Flame of Love* issues the most devastating criticism of incompetent spiritual directors who, instead of urging people to go through spiritual crisis, protect them from it, and try to create a ring road around the crisis. He calls them 'spiritual blacksmiths' who hammer and hammer at people to preserve them in their immaturities.

Some essential distinctions

It seems that there are close parallels between the spiritual tradition and therapy, but there are certain dangers in accepting too uncritically a clinical model for spirituality. Spiritual direction is not primarily concerned with states of emotional distress, or indeed with problem solving. It is very easy to misrepresent St John of the Cross in his writing about the 'dark night of the soul' as if he were talking about a state of clinical depression. St John of the Cross's teaching is that the dark night is the *normal* path to God. There is nothing pathological about it. It is the usual path which all Christians must take. It seems that there is a danger of creating what Lambourne called a 'hang-up theology', of seeing the spiritual path in terms of the identification and solution of problems. There is also a danger for therapy of creating an unreal world in which all problems are internalized. Perhaps one of the main reasons why we have psychiatry on the National Health Service is that there are many thousands of people in this country who, because they are under very severe pressure of housing, unemployment and other social and economic problems, cannot cope with their lives. Very often psychiatry is one way of helping not to solve these problems but to evade them.

Further, spiritual direction is rooted in the Christian community. It is not primarily a professional clinical phenomenon. It is very noticeable that, from the Hindu guru through to the Christian spiritual guide, there is a great insistence that the spiritual guide does not charge for his services. In fact, the authentic Hindu guru will most probably warn against the phoney gurus in the West who are distinguished by the fact that they charge fees! So, while it seems reasonable to speak of a clinical theology, it is a false conclusion to draw from this idea that theology is itself clinical. And here there is a real danger that the 'growth industry', so highly developed in the USA, may actually cash in on human suffering and distress and create a profitable undertaking. Anthony Clare ended his review of one of Thomas Szasz's books with the words, 'Psychiatry is alive and well and living in Beverley Hills.' There may be close parallels here with religion, for, whatever we may say about secularization, the human potential movement, growth groups, primal screams, and non-prophetic forms of contemplation and meditation are flourishing multimillion dollar industries. In the USA, and to a lesser extent here, they have come to be important parts of the culture of capitalism.

Spiritual direction is closely related to prophecy, and in this it has an essential social and critical dimension. It is not concerned with helping people to adjust, to adapt to the dubious value systems of society, but to question fundamentally those values. And this leads me to a final point: that, as well as learning from therapy, the Christian spiritual tradition must ask important questions of counselling, therapy, and the growth movement.

The Christian tradition must be seen to question – as have R. D. Laing and others – conventional models of sickness and sanity. Roszak says that we live with a 'diminished mode of consciousness', that we are 'unfinished animals seeking perfection'. He sees therapy as part of this movement: not merely the excavation of neurosis, but rather the opening up of the higher latent centres of the personality, and its evolution. If this is so, he argues, then it is essential to bring therapeutic work to the essentially 'well' person as a means of further growth, and he praises Gurdjieff as being the first person to realize the importance of therapy to the *well*. The point I wish to stress is that Roszak sees psychotherapy as a major conduit in our society for the transformation of consciousness. He believes that this new role for psychotherapy will actually lead to its own transformation as a discipline.

Christian spiritual theology needs to ask questions about the nature of consciousness and of personality, and to question some of the assumptions of physical-based psychiatry. It may well be true that religion has neglected the unconscious forces, but it would seem that a good deal of current health care and physical-based psychiatry is more or less determinist. One of the most disturbing examples of this trend was a letter to *The Times* on 9 January 1974 from some prison psychologists at Broadmoor. Writing of the treatment of abnormal offenders, they say: 'Psychology sees the entire range of human behaviour as determined by potentially explicable and predictable processes. Understanding these, for disposal and treatment, means that changes in behaviour can in principle be brought about.' This was in fact the gist of the British Psychological Society's evidence to the Butler Commission, and it seems to me to contain some very sinister political implications. Even more disturbing is the place of Professor Eysenck and the use that is made of his work in supporting reactionary political movements.

It seems that Christian theology needs to ask questions about the politics of therapy and counselling. What are therapy and counselling actually doing about the problems confronting human society? Are they in fact simply helping people to be well adjusted in a society whose fundamental values and interests remain unquestioned? Kathleen Heasman, in her *Introduction to Pastoral Counselling*, actually defines pastoral counselling as 'a relationship in which one person endeavours to help another to understand and to solve his difficulties of adjustment to society'.[7] This seems to me to be a highly dubious goal for the Christian, and although social work has been traditionally a conservative force, I am very pleased to see the rise of movements such as Radical Social Work and Red Therapy which are beginning to question the role of social work and counselling as instruments of social control.

It does seem, in fact, that therapy and counselling have one of the lowest levels of political awareness among the various disciplines. Thomas Szasz may be 'radical' in his theories of mental health, but he is certainly not radical in his conclusions which seem to be a psychiatric version of Milton Friedman's economics: therapy is simply available on the free-enterprise market for those who can pay for it. There seems to be a growing danger of the misuse of therapy and counselling in order to dodge and evade fundamental social and political issues, and this danger is not restricted to the Soviet Union. It is at this point that the Christian prophetic tradition of asking fundamental questions about justice in society is extremely important.

The real turning point in our dialogue will come when the search for inner wholeness and inner liberation comes into collision with the search for external wholeness and external liberation – when we see, in fact, that, in Roszak's words, 'the fate of the soul is the fate of the social order'.[8]

8

'Not Survival but Prophecy': The Future of Monasticism

The 'secular age'

'The problem for monasticism', wrote Thomas Merton, 'is not survival but prophecy.' Today we are being asked to consider the witness of the religious communities in the contemporary secular world, and I want therefore to begin by suggesting that we are not in fact in a secular world at all. The 1960s can be seen as an era when the mythology of secularization was widely accepted without adequate critical scrutiny. We were living, it was claimed, in what was called (somewhat tautologically) the 'secular age'. But today the myths of the '60s are coming under heavy fire, and many of those who were involved in the Christian movements of thought in the '60s have begun to have different thoughts.

> We came increasingly to believe that all this was true. Even our religious establishments, our various Vaticans, came to believe that it was true. They have been operating, more or less, on this assumption ever since. The assumption is not true; it has been discredited not by theologians but by events. In fact we were entering – not a secularized age as we thought – we were entering then an age of incredible religiosity.[1]

In similar vein speaks the Chicago sociologist Andrew Greeley. Arguing against the conventional wisdom of the '60s, Greeley suggests that 'the basic human religious needs and the basic religious functions have not changed very notably since the late Ice Age.' Religion, he says, is not in a state of collapse:

> . . . the religious crises of the intellectual community by no means reflect the religious situation of the mass of the people. 'Western man', 'modern man', 'technological man',

> 'secular man', are to be found, for the most part, only on university campuses, and increasingly only among senior faculty members, as the students engage in witchcraft, astrology, and other bizarre religious practices.[2]

Now a secular situation implies that the religious categories are dead or obsolete. Man gets on OK without God. But this does not seem to be the situation in our society. Certainly it is true that conventional religion is dying, though in some places much more slowly than in others. On the other hand, religion and spirituality are very much alive, but they have been 'privatized', that is, banished to the private sector, to the realm of the personal. Religions have become commodities, and have come to be restricted in scope so that they do not disturb, threaten, or affect the prevailing social order. Survival, even expansion, certainly not prophecy.

Idolatry

In the Old Testament, the prophetic attack on social systems was framed in the language of oppression, fornication, and rebellion. Grinding the faces of the poor, playing the harlot, refusing to hear the Word of the Lord: anti-poor, anti-chaste, anti-obedient. And the whole syndrome was identified as one of idolatry. And our society is more than anything else an idolatrous society. Theodore Roszak has pointed out that idolatry is a mistaken ontology, grounded in a flawed consciousness, a diminished form of consciousness, a narrowing of perspective and of vision. We live, he claims, in a wasteland of the spirit, so that we have become 'the only idolatrous culture in the history of mankind.'[3]

I want broadly to accept Roszak's description and to suggest that we are in a period of severe spiritual deprivation. Moreover, in this society we see the antitype of the monastic community with its anti-vows. So it is that poverty, chastity, and obedience have become demonic, the exact opposite of the vows of religion, the symbols now of oppression and idolatry. First, the anti-vow of poverty, a commitment to inequalities of wealth and power, concentrated financial power, growing areas of poverty and deprivation. And, let us note, these are not simply pockets of accidental poverty, unfortunate blots on the urban landscape, but essential and inevitable poverty, so long as the maldistribution of resources and the imbalance in society remain. Secondly, the anti-vow of chastity, a commitment to dehumanization, to what Marcuse called 'one-dimensional man', to the denial of human sexuality. Surely not, cry the critics, how can anyone seriously maintain that ours is a desexualized society? Oversexed, perhaps. Yet in fact the apparent explosion of 'liberated' sexuality is far less significant than the prevalence of sexual ignorance in our society, a prevalence to which any Samaritan, any marriage guidance counsellor, in fact, anyone working at the personal level with individuals and couples would testify. The surface manifestations of apparently 'liberated' sexuality are, for the most part, merely the pathetic admission of the lack of it. There is, rather, a dulling of the feelings: sexuality is banished to the bedroom and to the genital area. We can no longer say, with Julian of Norwich, that our substance and our sensuality are in God. We are suffering from what St Thomas Aquinas termed *insensibilitas* and which he stigmatized as a vice. Thirdly, the anti-vow of obedience, for we have become an increasingly authoritarian and repressive society, the society of the corporate state where it is the 'yes-men' who prosper. In such a society, claimed Thomas Merton in his 'Devout Meditation on the Death of Adolf Eichmann', the sane ones are those who are not plagued by doubt, who obey orders without question.[4] And the most sinister fact about these anti-vows is that they are not even freely made: they are merely accepted as part of the way things are. So there is an anti-contemplation, a disease of partial perception, or of no perception at all.

The monastic role

It is perhaps becoming clear how I see the role of the religious orders in such a society, and I draw very much on the thought of two recent writers: Thomas Merton, in a wide range of his works, and Adrian Hastings in his essay on 'marginality' in a recent collection.[5] Merton saw the role of the modern monk to be that of social critic, questioner, one who is concerned essentially with the 'unmasking of illusion',[6] In a now famous paper which he gave at Bangkok on the day he died, Merton claimed that 'the monk is essentially someone who takes up a critical attitude towards the contemporary world and its structures'.[7] Earlier, in his *Contemplative Prayer*, Merton had argued that this age of crisis, revolution, and struggle was one which particularly called for 'the special searching and questioning which are the work of the monk in his meditation and prayer'.[8] The monk, in Merton's view, is 'a marginal person . . . who withdraws deliberately to the margin of society with a view to deepening fundamental human experience.'[9] It should be noted – as Merton himself noted from time to time – that if this is true, then the monk's place must be alongside other marginal people who are in that position, not through voluntary choice, but through the operation of what I have termed the anti-vows. Ironically, one of the first uses of the term 'marginal men' occurred in 1960 in the study by Ruth Glass, the urban sociologist, of the Notting Hill race riots of 1958,[10] and it was the same writer, in 1965, who warned of the formation of 'ghettoes of "displaced persons" – of all kinds and shades . . . in the metropolitan area.'[11] Professor Glass wrote with her North Kensington study very much in mind. If we put together Merton and Glass, it would seem that, whether by accident or design, St Andrew's House is rightly placed for marginal people!* Adrian Hastings pushed this notion of marginality further. One of the essential features of the monastic life, he argues, should be the sense of social non-status. But monasticism is rarely faithful to its calling. 'The nun and the monk should be the great protesters . . . They should be God's clearest face in the world.'[12]

From the margins of society, what role has the monastic community to play within the society of the anti-vows? Its role is surely to witness to the life-style which is the reverse of that which I have described. There is a *social role*, the commitment to *koinonia*, to the common life which is the sign of the resurrection and of the new order. It is not an attack on materialism which is needed today so much as an attack on false spirituality which denies that the social life of the City of God ('I know not, O, I know not, what social joys are there!')

* This was originally given as a lecture at St Andrew's House, Notting Hill.

has anything to do with this order.

The *humanist role*, the commitment to *sarx*, to the sacredness of the flesh, to a way of loving which does not shun sexuality but deepens and transforms it.

The *political role*, the commitment to *krisis*, to the judgement which obedience to the Father necessarily brings upon the false orders of this age, the judgement which makes contemplation a subversive activity by its nature.

I believe therefore that the monastic vows, at every point, represent a rejection of, and a witness against, the values and idols of our society.

The dangers to monastic witness

But if this is so, why is it not evident? Clearly there are some central theological questions which affect the issue. One of the urgent issues here is that of eschatology. I don't think that any Christian has ever doubted that the life of the Kingdom of God is one of anarchist communism, that is, of the putting down of rule, authority, and power, and the sharing of all spiritual and material goods. The doubt has been about whether this reality is all in the future or not! The witness of the monastic life is in part an assertion that the life of the Kingdom, of the new age, is being lived now, that the powers of the age to come are already operative, but the central theological task of relating the life of the communities to the life of the world remains. Here I can only pursue the more modest task of pointing to four areas where there are real dangers to the authenticity of the monastic witness.

One danger is that it may simply be absorbed, ritualized. So poverty becomes a euphemism, celibacy becomes preciousness and eccentricity, and obedience becomes evasion of responsibility. In other words, the vows cease to be a testimony and become the private pursuit of those who are so inclined. They are the vows of a called minority, they do not speak to the world. So the world is absolved of responsibility for poverty, chastity, and obedience in its whole life; the monks and nuns witness to them at the margins of society instead. It is easy then for the orders to receive with gratitude this role of accepted eccentrics, absorbed minorities, what

Father Stanton once called 'established strangers and endowed pilgrims'. So in holy poverty, one woos and cultivates the wealthy aristocratic lady oblates and preaches good news to the public schools. But what does it mean to prophesy about poverty in these situations, in the world of Notting Hill riots and educational inequalities? Woe to those who are at ease in Zion! Woe to those who are at ease anywhere!

There is a danger of becoming enslaved to cultures, dead or living, past or present, mainstream, subcultures or counter-cultures. So the community may simply preserve old cultural patterns, quaint customs and habits (in both senses!), and become a kind of ritual re-enactment of the old order, losing touch with society as it is now. In this connection, it must be stressed that there is a growing need for, and a growing struggle to express, experimental forms of community life in urban areas, and there is a need for these to draw upon, and to be linked with, the resources of the great spiritual traditions, and the long established orders. Or the community may grasp with uncritical and romantic enthusiasm at the latest fashion, and that can be a form of slavery too.

There is the danger that the community loses contact with the places of vision, loses the ability to see clearly because it is standing in the wrong place. Most communities are middle-class institutions, and are geared to a refined, middle-class, *Guardian*-reading community outside. The literature which is published is aimed at this section of the public. Perhaps the literature which is read in monasteries and convents is also of this type. What about the *Daily Mirror*, *Capital Radio*, *Time Out* and *Melody Maker*, not to mention *Socialist Worker* or *Gay News*? Are they read by monks and nuns? Yet how can one perceive the signs of the times if one fails to have one ear to the ground? I don't think that this remoteness from the places of vision is a disease which is peculiar to communities, and indeed it is not most acute in communities. Bishops and academic theologians are more plagued by it, for how can they speak prophetically and with a right sense of perspective when they are invariably so far removed from the vantage points of the mass of the population? If, as Merton says the monk's role is to listen carefully to the hidden and neglected voices of the world, then the place on which you stand is very important indeed. For if you are in the wrong place, you will not hear, and you will not see. I want therefore to make a plea that the urban areas and the inner city should not lose their contemplatives, for they are desperately needed there.

The most serious danger is that the community might be tempted to abandon its essentially contemplative role for something else, and by doing so cease to be able to give the world that which it most needs and most lacks – clarity of vision. Many years ago, Jung said that the role of the clergy was to teach people the art of seeing. I believe that this is a central characteristic of both priesthood and monasticism: to awaken vision, awareness, insight, contemplation. The worst thing that could happen therefore is that communities and priests succumb to the temptation to activism and 'doing good', and that, because of this, the sun goes down on the prophets. Because there will be no prophecy if there is no vision; and if there is no vision, the people will perish.

9

The Charismatic Movement and the Demons

The question of exorcism

The question of exorcism and the demonic has been brought to the fore in recent years by two sets of factors. The first is the widespread, though unevenly documented, upsurge of interest in the occult among the young and the not-so-young.[1] The second is the occurrence of several horrifying instances of deaths in which exorcism was involved.[2] As a result there has been a good deal of sensational publicity leading to demands that exorcism should be banned. Many Christians have reacted by an unwillingness to entertain the idea of evil forces or of their oppression of human beings altogether, while some groups, notably some Christians associated with the charismatic renewal, have become obsessed with the demonic and with deliverance ministries. The question is therefore an important one which calls for theological scrutiny.

The demonic in the New Testament

In the New Testament the symbol of the demonic is used of warped institutions in the ordering of society. '"Satan" and "Beelzebub" are names for warped institutions.'[3] Behind the 'powers that be' in the world, there are *angeloi*, *daimoniai*, *archai*, *exousiai*, there are the 'world rulers of this present darkness', the 'rudiments of the world'.[4] In the New Testament, exorcism is both a theological and a political concept, involving both the activity of God's power and the setting free of individuals and communities from slavery to the structures of a fallen world. It is very probable that the demonology which is assumed by the New Testament writers derives from the widespread astral beliefs of the period, and there is a central theme of cosmic warfare, involving heaven as well as earth, and involving a great army of invisible beings.[5] 'It is these invisible beings who in some way . . . stand behind what occurs in the world'.[6]

The theme of cosmic warfare is a constant one throughout the Christian tradition and is closely linked with the coming of the Kingdom of God.[7] Thus in the Gospels exorcisms are 'signs of the coming of the Kingdom'.[8] 'If I cast out devils by the Spirit of God (Luke: the finger of God), then the Kingdom of God has come to you.' (Matthew 12:28; Luke 11:20.) Moreover, it is clear that the liberation of men from slavery to the demonic powers is not something which is peripheral to the Gospels, but is rather 'an altogether central article of faith'.[9] 'Most of us', wrote Harvey Cox, 'would prefer to forget that for many of his contemporaries, Jesus' exorcism was in no way peripheral, but stood at the heart of his work.'[10] In Galilee, exorcism was certainly 'his main occupation'.[11] Norman Perrin summed up the conclusions of most modern scholarship:[12]

> The evidence for exorcism as a feature of the ministry of Jesus is very strong indeed: exorcisms are to be found in every strata of the synoptic tradition, and the ancient Jewish texts regard Jesus as a miracle worker, i.e. an exorcist. The present writer vividly remembers a conversation with Ernst Käsemann, at that time in Göttingen, in which that leading member of the 'Bultmann school' exclaimed that he had no choice, if he wished to remain a historian, but to accept the historicity of the tradition that Jesus was an exorcist. Today this would be a widely accepted consensus of critical opinion.

However, it is also clear that the cases cited in the Synoptic writers were cases of disease for which we today would offer a quite different kind of explanation and description: mental disturbance, epilepsy, convulsions, dumbness and blindness. What is crucial, therefore, is that in all cases, physical and mental healing was accompanied by the setting free of the person from oppression, from those forces, both within him and without, which stunted and distorted his humanity. It is this liberation, this achievement of the freedom of man to be fully human, which is the central purpose of the Christian Gospel. The contemporary demonology expressed the oppression in terms of evil spirits, but the reality of oppression is still present, and it is this which is portrayed in the demonic symbol.

In St Paul's writings, Christ is said to have conquered the powers, and Paul in Romans looks forward to the liberation of the entire created order, perhaps including the powers themselves, from oppression and slavery. The principalities and powers cannot separate the Christian from the love of God. They are to be dethroned and subjugated, and between them and the church there is a continuing conflict. But Christ has already disarmed them and triumphed over them.[13] Paul took over the symbolism of apocalyptic writers but while they see the powers as heavenly angels, Paul sees them as 'structures of earthly existence'.[14] It is doubtful if he sees them as personal beings. Rather, as Berkhof has written:[15]

> In the light of God's action Paul perceived that mankind is not composed of loose individuals, but that structures, orders, forms of existence, or whatever they be called, are given us as a part of creaturely life and that these are involved, as much as men themselves, in the history of creation, fall, preservation, reconciliation, and consummation. This insight he expressed in the terms and concepts of his time.

We are not bound today, says Berkhof, by Paul's language, but his insight maintains its validity and relevance for us.[16]

The misunderstanding of exorcism

This teaching about cosmic warfare and the struggle of Christ against the powers is the essential background to the discussion of exorcism. Today there seem to be two common misconceptions on the subject, and they are reflected in most recent writing, including the Open Letter of the '65 theologians' of 1975. The first is the view that exorcism is inseparable from, and limited to, the concept of possession. In fact, in the traditional practice of the western church, as well as in psychiatric experience, possession is very rare. Dom Robert Petitpierre, an Anglican monk with considerable experience in this field, has claimed that the notion of possession is 'quite hopelessly overdrawn', and that twelve cases in England is a maximum.[17] 'Demonic control of any person is extremely rare . . . Of all the cases of paranormal phenomena I have dealt with, now running into several hundreds, I can recall only one case of genuine demonic control.' Possession then is 'extremely rare, estimated at no more than 1 per cent of all the cases coming forward.'[18]

Of course, the 'possession syndrome' is well-known. Freud, in an essay of 1923, noted the similarity between the demonological theory of possession and the psychoanalytic theory of hysteria. '. . . The neuroses of these early times emerge in demonological trappings . . . The states of possession correspond to our neuroses . . . In our eyes the demons are bad and reprehensible wishes, derivatives of instinctual impulses that have been repudiated and repressed.'[19] A more recent psychiatric writer, Rollo May, has said that demonic possession is simply 'the traditional name throughout history for psychosis'.[20] Since the work of Jung in the whole area of the unconscious and its symbolism, we cannot claim that the categories of theology and psychopathology are alternatives and mutually exclusive.[21] R. D. Laing has pointed out that medical terms describe and do not explain. 'To say that Statement A "Possessed by a demon" is explained by "He is mentally disturbed" – it is not an explanation. It is simply another way of talking that doesn't in fact explain anything.'[22]

The solemn exorcism of the possessed thus is rare and has always in practice represented a small range of cases. The idea of exorcism is a much wider one. It is certainly not of medieval origin as has been claimed. Indeed, it was an integral element of the baptismal liturgy from the earliest times.[23] Many of the Fathers refer to the drowning of the demons in the waters. As early as Hippolytus, there is a pre-baptismal exorcism, while the rejection of the dominion of Satan is a central element in the baptismal teaching of St Cyril of Jerusalem and St Gregory of Nyssa. 'Exorcisms therefore are the beginning of the fight that constitutes the first and essential dimension of Christian life . . . Liberation from demonic power is the beginning of man's restoration.'[24] It might be argued that the watering down of this element in modern Anglicanism has had serious repurcussions insofar as it has aided the process of compromise with much that belongs to the realm of darkness and of avoidance of any real conflict with the devil and the fallen world-order.[25] In the modern Roman baptismal rite, the Prayer of Exorcism is a prayer that God who sent his only Son into the world to cast out the power of Satan, the spirit of evil, to rescue man from the kingdom of darkness and to bring him into the splendour of his Kingdom of Grace, would set the candidate free from original sin, make him a temple of God's glory, and send him the Holy Spirit. Thus exorcism is one element in a total liturgy of deliverance and healing in which the realm of evil is rejected and man is restored to the divine realm.

The second error is to isolate the demonic from its origins in political theology, that is, in the theology of structural sin. So the demonic ceases to be a powerful symbol of deeply rooted evil in the created order, and becomes a literal description of entities within individuals. In this process of pseudo-spiritualisation, the real demons in the world are often missed. It is striking that Black Theology, a movement rooted in the experience of human racial oppression and of the structures of injustice, has rediscovered the true sense of the demonic. Thus one writer comments:[26]

> Already the demons are being named. The enemy is being identified. Its names are legion. Racism is a demon. Poverty is a demon. Powerlessness is a demon. Self-depreciation is a demon. And those who prop them up are demonic in effect. A strategy of liberation includes a ministry of exorcism, the naming and casting out of demons.

Similarly, James Cone explains that 'the reference to Satan and demons is not simply an outmoded first-century world-view', but rather brings out the scandal of the Gospel.

> . . . the exorcisms disclose that God in Jesus has brought liberation to the poor and the wretched of the land, and that liberation is none other than the overthrow of everything that is against the fulfilment of their humanity. The scandal

is that the gospel means liberation, that this liberation comes to the poor, and that it gives them the strength and the courage to break the conditions of servitude.[27]

The charismatic renewal and its dangers

The exorcisms thus stand for the setting free of human beings from slavery and oppression, from the principalities and powers of the fallen world. Today, however, the charismatic movement, or, to use a less emotive and less loaded term, Neo-Pentecostalism, seems to have lent itself to the distortion of the demonic symbol, and at times to a harmful and very unbalanced pre-occupation with demonology. Cardinal Suenens has spoken of 'demonomania' and of 'the uncontrolled popularisation and proliferation of exorcisms in certain charismatic groups'.[28] There are a number of reasons why the charismatic movement is particularly open to this type of abuse. Biblical literalism of an extremely unintelligent type is very common, if not the norm, among Pentecostals, and this can lead to irrational and often absurd interpretations of biblical concepts. Of course, it is often argued today that biblical literalism is not essential in those who share the 'charismatic experience' but is rather a hangover from the theological superstructure of classical Pentecostalism. This is strictly true, but in actual practice the group expression and interpretations of the experience do seem to go hand in hand with traditional Pentecostal use of the Bible. Cardinal Suenens links the irresponsible use of exorcism directly with 'a fundamentalist reading of holy Scripture'.[29]

The absence of a sacramental life in some of the traditions which have been affected by Neo-Pentecostalism seems to have led to an unbalanced stress on such ritual forms as exorcism or speaking in tongues which then come to assume the status of pseudo-sacraments. The routine sacramental means of deliverance are under-valued, and emphasis is placed on the unusual and the sensational. To some extent, the spread of the charismatic movement is a reaction against the dreary anti-sacramentalist types of Protestantism which have marred so much of western Christianity for many years, and a desperate search for ways of expressing the inarticulate elements in worship which the non-sacramental, over-cerebral style has obscured or ignored.

The individualistic theology which lies behind most forms of Pentecostalism leads to a view of evil which is theologically unsound, pastorally dangerous, and socio-politically usually right-wing. That is not to deny that evangelical Christians often discover, through the charismatic movement, a new understanding of community and of the social dimensions of the faith. But this understanding of the *Christian* community is not usually associated with a grasp of the social forces within the wider world. So there is a tendency to isolate evil within the sphere of the private, and it is this sphere which comes to be seen as par excellence the territory of the demons. Pastorally such views can lead to serious mis-handling of people, and there are now many cases of disturbed individuals who have fallen into the hands of enthusiastic exorcists and healers of Pentecostal outlook, and whose condition has subsequently become much worse. The psychiatrist Jack Dominian has suggested that 'the Pentecostal movement . . . has an inbuilt bias in attracting those who are emotionally disturbed or truly mentally ill.'[30] What may happen then if a disturbed individual identifies his or her condition with demons and is then brought into contact with a Pentecostal minister who is obsessed with demonology?

> If such a man or woman, however, encounters a clergyman who is obsessed with the presence of the devil in the singular or the plural, then the most disastrous collusion and consequences can ensue and occasionally do so. After the tragedy of last year 1975 much was heard about the need for great cooperation between Pentecostal groups and doctors and much greater supervision of exorcism. All this is essential if the Christian community is not to become associated with any further tragedies. But in my view, necessary as such cooperation is, it avoids the fundamental examination of the psychological make-up of members of all Christian denominations who are so pre-occupied with the devil and who are constantly looking for his presence. I have no doubt at all that such a pre-occupation is in fact pathological, and the correct Christian perspective and

doctrine is distorted through the psychological make-up of such fundamental leanings and belief.[31]

Sadly, but not altogether surprisingly, it seems that a high proportion of ministers and others who become pre-occupied with exorcism soon become obsessed with it, and may themselves become psychologically unhinged as well as theologically heretical. A recent Roman Catholic memorandum warned that 'excessive pre-occupation with the demonic and an indiscriminate exercise of deliverance ministries is based upon a distortion of the biblical evidence and is pastorally harmful'.[32] The recent comments by Cardinal Suenens have reinforced the same point.[33] Of course, not all these theological emphases and pastoral excesses are present in all sections of the charismatic movement, and there is considerable criticism of them within the renewal itself. The problem is, however, that there may not be the theological resources within Neo-Pentecostalism to avoid these errors without a major theological critique of the renewal itself.

Moreover, in terms of social and political thought and action, there is a serious danger that the false demonology of the Pentecostal tradition will in practice lead to a blindness to, and therefore indirectly a support for, the really demonic forces in the world. It has been claimed that the 'charismatic renewal has the potential for developing a far more solid, long-term, radical commitment to social justice at all levels than any other movement in the church',[34] and the highly respected authority on Pentecostalism, W. J. Hollenweger, has argued that there are radicalising trends in white Pentecostal movements.[35] One cannot simply write off such views, but the evidence from Britain does seem to be heavily against them. If anything, the spread of Neo-Pentecostalism in Britain seems to have aided the general shift to the political right, the suspicion of working-class movements, and the spiritual defence of a dying order. Evidence from other parts of the world reinforces the view that concern with demons actually diverts attention from the real conflict with evil in the world. Thus the Asian Christian leader T. K. Thomas:[36]

We have freedom in many Asian countries to preach the gospel, to speak in tongues, to conduct healing ministries,

> and even to cast out evil spirits – as long as the gospel does not disturb, the tongues do not make sense, the healing does not extend to the diseases of the body politic, and the spirits are the ones with no visibility. We rejoice, against Jesus' explicit injunction, that the spirits are subject to us: and leave the principalities and powers strictly alone.

Worst of all, there seems to be a fundamental irrationality and lack of theological and intellectual seriousness which prevents any real assessment of these dangers and trends within the movement. The Pentecostal experience often seems to lead to a sentimentality and immaturity in human relationships, and an abdication of hard theological analysis in favour of pietism. In a society as complex as ours, the retreat into pietistic forms of religion was predictable, and there are strong indications that the charismatic movement is only one way of evading problems in the real world which are too difficult to handle. In terms of social ethics, the movement is virtually barren. In its social and political witness, it is either very trivial, or positively reactionary, identifying as demonic the very forces which are working for change and justice in society. In general, there is a loss of wholeness of Christian truth in many sections of the movement to such an extent that the description 'heretical' might not be too strong. Certainly the heretical demonology is merely one facet of a wider breakdown.

10
Is There a New Religious Fascism?

I want to examine the thesis that there is in Britain today a kind of 'creeping fascism', and to discuss the possible connections with Christian theology or its distortions. I shall divide my argument into three sections. First, what do we mean by fascism? Secondly, what kind of relationship is possible between Christian, or quasi-Christian, ideas and fascist ideology? Thirdly, what are the danger signs in Britain today? I do not propose to look at the complex problems of the apparent resurgence of Catholic fascism in Europe, or its links with the Lefevbre movement, though that phenomenon is clearly worthy of fuller examination.

The nature of fascism

The definition of fascism presents a number of notoriously difficult problems.[1] From the time when fascism emerged in Italy until the 1930s there was little attempt to view the movement as an international phenomenon. It was the success of National Socialism in Germany which brought the question of an international perspective on fascism into prominence, and between 1933 and 1945 there was a very considerable literature. This literature

> engendered the major interpretations of Fascism that dominated and to a degree continue to dominate our politics and thought: Fascism as the product of a moral crisis in European society during the first half of the Twentieth Century; Fascism as the result of retarded and untypical economic development and national unification in European countries such as Italy and Germany; and the Marxist notion that Fascism was the senescent or dying stage of

> capitalism or at the very least the final product of class struggle.[2]

Complaints about the indiscriminate and loose use of the term fascism are now almost as common and as predictable as is the use of the term itself. It is often used to describe racialist groups of the 'ultra-right', or used of almost any authoritarian or repressive system or individual. There are sometimes references to 'left-wing fascism', a concept which goes back historically to Reich, who used the term 'red fascism', and beyond.[3] Sometimes fascism is seen as a conspiracy, a plot, sometimes as a present reality. Sometimes it is identified with racialism, racial violence, increased police powers, authoritarianism, repressive legislation, and so on. All these, of course, are elements in a process of 'creeping fascism', but the fascist state is far more than all of them. It is a phenomenon of industrial society in severe socio-economic crisis, confronted by the threat of collapse on the one hand, and by the threat of socialism on the other, and containing a very frightened and threatened middle class.[4]

There seem to be three common perspectives on the analysis of fascism today. The first virtually equates fascism with racism and racist doctrines, and tends to see the anti-semitic character of Nazism as its defining characteristic. So today's fascist and quasi-fascist movements are easily identifiable: they are essentially racist movements. I believe this view to be seriously mistaken because one has to distinguish between levels of racism, and failure to do this merely increases confusion. I want to distinguish between three levels which I will call *racism*, *racialism*, and *quasi-racism*.[5] *Racism* is the systematic ideology of racial superiority, embodied in the law and structures of the state, as in Nazi Germany, and only existing in its full form today in South Africa. *Racialism* is the actual unequal treatment of various racial groups: this exists in most societies, irrespective of their ideology or lack of it. *Quasi-racism* occurs where there is some implicit doctrine of racial superiority, such as we find in our society. Now all these phenomena are different, but none of them can strictly be called fascism. They can all exist without fascism, and fascism without them. Certainly all these forms of racial oppression had their origin in the colonial period, for the enslavement and proletarianizing of whole continents needed some ideology or philosophy of inferiority to justify it. But racialism can and does exist within liberal frameworks, even though its philosophy is opposed to that of liberalism. It is when the underlying incompatibility of liberalism and capitalism is revealed that some form of state repression becomes the only way to maintain state power. But paradoxically, at a certain level of economic activity, it may be found that racism itself is incompatible with *successful* capitalism. So one black writer has argued that the institutional racism which was fostered by the British Government in its immigration laws is now being attacked by that Government through its Race Relations Acts, through its Commission for Racial Equality, and so on, as part of a policy of strengthening state power. So 'it finds it more profitable to abandon the idea of the superiority of race in order to promote the idea of the superiority of capital. Racism dies in order that capital might survive.'[6] So violence against racial minorities, and racist ideology, may be factors in the growth of fascism, but they are by no means the only form that this can take.

In recent years, there has been 'renewed interest in the problem of fascism',[7] and models of fascism derived from the 1930s are under attack. One of the best-known and most controversial attempts to redefine fascism is that of the black activist George Jackson who virtually equates fascism with increased state repression. He then argues that after the economic crisis of the last great depression, fascism did emerge and consolidate itself in its most advanced form in the United States. He insists that 'the final definition of fascism is still open simply because it is still a developing movement'.[8] Yet its essential features are clear. It involves the constitution of a new form of state to control the means of production and consumption within capitalism, and to do this it needs a repressive machinery and an ideological apparatus. Jackson believes that 'pure fascism, absolute totalitarianism, is not possible', but he sees the growth of the repressive state machine as a response to the threat of socialism. In order to establish this repressive machine it is essential to dismantle the working class movement. Where it is not possible, as in the

1930s, to crush the working class movement by starvation or reduced wage levels, some new method of control is needed, for example, the transformation of trade unions into state police. So the possibility of private armies under state control becomes a viable tool of an emerging fascist state.

Against Jackson's view is a third view, which I want broadly to accept, which is that fascism is growing, that there is a clear tendency towards the repressive corporate state, but that we are not at the final point yet. The transition from the strong state to true fascism occurs at the point at which a terrorist dictatorship is imposed and all opposition is crushed. Only then, in my view, can we speak of true fascism, but this must not prevent us from identifying the signs and indications on the way. Carl Schmidt's study of the corporate state showed how rapidly Mussolini's movement grew. In 1920 Mussolini had only 17,000 supporters: within two years they had grown to 450,000, and he was able to set up a fascist trade union centre with 800,000 adherents.[9] Mussolini's article in the *Enciclopedia Italiana* in 1933 remains a normative description of fascist state control.

> Fascism is opposed to socialism which clings rigidly to class war in the historic evolution and ignores the unity of the state which moulds the classes into a single moral and economic reality. In the same way fascism is opposed to the unions of the labouring classes. But within the orbit of the state with ordinative functions, the real needs which give rise to the socialist movement and to the forming of labour unions are emphatically recognized by Fascism and are given their full expression in the corporative system which conciliates every interest in the unity of the state.[10]

I feel therefore that the distinction between the *strong repressive state* and the *fascist state* needs to be maintained. In no way does this involve underrating the seriousness of the former. I shall call the tendencies to move from one to the other 'creeping fascism', and it is in this context that we need to view the increasing signs of anti-communist and anti-class struggle campaigns and tendencies, as well as calls for national unity, critiques of liberalism, of the trades unions, and so on.

Christian fundamentalism and the ultra-right

I want now to turn to the place of the Christian religion or its distortions in providing ideological backing for fascist movements or tendencies, and I want first to discuss the place of biblical fundamentalism in relation to the politics of the ultra-right. The subject of biblical fundamentalism has been reopened in the recent weighty study by James Barr.[11] Here I want to restrict the discussion to one facet: the connection between a crude fundamentalist theology and support for ultra-right-wing political positions. Clearly, on the historical evidence, there is a close connection, and it is particularly marked in the United States. It has, for example, been shown that right-wing extremist groups are strongest in the United States in those states which once officially repudiated Darwinism, though it needs to be remembered that these were also the most deprived states.[12] The study by Lipset and Raab[13] of the American ultra-right over the last two hundred years brings out the close links between the cruder forms of fundamentalism and the emergence of anti-semitic, anti-communist and anti-liberal political groups, such as the Ku Klux Klan, the John Birch Society, the Christian Crusade, and so on, though they emphasize that 'the congruence of Protestant fundamentalism and moralism with right-wing extremism is in one sense a historical accident' and that 'religious fundamentalism does not create right-wing extremism'.[14] It is rather that reactionary backlash movements seek an aggressive moralistic stance and an ideology, and Protestant fundamentalism seems to be ideally suited to that purpose. Thus 'there is general agreement that the Protestant clergy were disproportionately represented in the membership and leadership of the Klan.'[15] A detailed analysis of the membership of the KKK in Knoxville, Tennessee, showed that 71 per cent belonged to Baptist churches and 24 per cent to Methodist ones.[16] A study of the American 'radical right' in 1967 showed that nearly half of the extreme right-wingers interviewed were affiliated to fundamentalist churches.[17] Support for George Wallace similarly came largely from fundamentalist Christians as did much of that for Reagan.[18]

Of course, it is true that 'although Puritanism is probably

one of the main sources of American intolerance, there are certainly many other elements which have contributed to its continuance in American life.'[19] Yet it remains clear that crude fundamentalism and ultra-right-wing politics are still closely correlated in many places. David Reimers in his study *White Protestantism and the Negro* (1965) showed how in the southern states a crude fundamentalism provided a theological defence of racism. 'Protestantism helped pave the way for the capitulation to racism at the turn of the century.'[20] By the 1870s the Southern Baptist Convention was virtually an all-white church. 'If anything, southern Protestant leaders were in the vanguard of those urging white supremacy and racial segregation . . . In their eyes the Protestant God was a racist God; few saw any incompatibility between white supremacy and Christianity.'[21] The history of American revivalism provides a depressing picture in terms of its social outlook. Finney was ambivalent on slavery and refused to abolish segregated seating in his chapel. Moody told the unemployed in New York in the depression that their plight was due to their sins, and saw the conversion of the lower classes as necessary for the prevention of civil disorder. Billy Sunday denounced the Fatherhood of God and the Brotherhood of Man as 'the worst rot dug out of hell'.[22] As late as 1955, Carl Henry, regarded by many writers as a radical evangelical, was speaking of Christianity as a force to 'safeguard free enterprise from perversion'.[23]

It is out of this revivalist tradition that Billy Graham emerged. Graham has had a very major influence on evangelicals in the UK, and it is important therefore to be clear about his beliefs. It ought also to be remembered that, to many fundamentalists, he is a dangerous liberal and an ecumenist: in terms of American religious culture, he is in the mainstream, not on the fringe, of the revivalist tradition. Graham once claimed (on the basis of the Book of Revelation) that heaven would be about the same size as the state of Florida, though governed rather differently! He still rejects the theory of evolution as the work of Satan, and combines a crude fundamentalism with a commitment to the American way of life. Through the McCarthy period, he was referring to 'rats and termites' and praising McCarthy for exposing 'the pinks, the lavenders and the reds'. His pro-Nixon sympathies are well known, and he followed very closely the Nixon line in social policy on such issues as anti-pornography, anti-communism and (after 1972) when Nixon switched to the 'generation of peace' language, Billy Graham followed him. Graham's theology is heavily against the politics of the left, and he has claimed that 'we are too tolerant of those people who are against the basic principles of this country', naming specifically communists and adulterers.[24]

One could go on indefinitely. The point I wish to stress is that the tradition of fundamentalist revivalism in the USA has in the main led to the association of evangelical Christianity with right-wing political positions. This was expressed by Athol Gill in the symposium on the Lausanne Covenant in 1974. Speaking of evangelical attitudes since the 1920s he wrote:

> During the 1920s evangelicals, reacting to the extremes of the 'social gospel' and reflecting the middle-class values of the society in which they flourished, reversed their earlier interest in social action and concentrated their efforts almost solely upon denouncing personal evils and proclaiming individual salvation. Conservative in their theology, evangelicals became increasingly conservative in their approach to politics, economics, culture and social issues generally (even though the major thrust of their theological position should have pressed them in quite a different direction). They aligned themselves with right-wing political parties which were seeking to maintain the status quo and so frequently became deaf to the cries of the underprivileged and disenfranchized. The 'American Way of Life' was regarded as the epitome of Christianity as evangelicalism became almost inextricably bound up with western culture. To support the system was to proclaim the Gospel, to challenge it was to challenge God. The prophetic voice was muted, if not silenced, and involvement in social and political movements which sought to change existing structures was identified as 'liberalism' and even 'communism'. These were the dark ages of evangelicalism![25]

I would suggest that those ages are not yet past, and that

today, as in an earlier period, fundamentalism provides a basis for religious intolerance.

Christians and Nazism

I want now to turn to one of the most disturbing features of Christian history this century: the capitulation of thousands of German Christians to Nazism. In 1941 the Ecclesiastical Council of the German Evangelical Church, in a telegram, assured Hitler of 'the unshakeable loyalty and readiness for service of the entire evangelical Christendom in Germany'. The Führer had, they said, 'staved off the Bolshevist peril', and was now calling the nation to arms against 'the deadly enemy of all order and all European-Christian civilization'. Many Christians saw Hitler as a great moral crusader and saviour who had come, as he said, 'to complete the work of Luther'.[26] I want to identify two features which aided the surrender to Hitler. First, the collapse of any true prophetic social tradition, and the concern instead with the Church's status, power, and privilege at the cost of its integrity. Secondly, the defective theology which deprived the Church of the spiritual resources for resistance.

The danger is seen clearly in the situation of the Roman Church. Guenter Lewy in *The Catholic Church and Nazi Germany* (1964)[27] shows how Rome, dominated by the fear of atheistic communism, was led to tolerate the fascist states. Indeed, not only to tolerate but often to justify the fascist ideology. Catholic social ideals as set forth in the encyclicals of Leo XIII and Pius XI, claimed Christopher Dawson in 1936, 'have far more affinity with Fascism than with those of either Liberalism or Socialism.'[28] The Church, said Pius XI in 1933, the year Hitler came to power, 'does not find any difficulty in adapting herself to various civil institutions, be they monarchic or republican, aristocratic or democratic.'[29] In fact many Christians, Catholic and Protestant, found no difficulty in adapting themselves to Nazism, even to the extent of preaching sermons from which all Christian dogma had been removed.[30]

The Roman Catholic background to the alliance with fascism goes back a long way. The early social encyclicals were marked by an intense fear of socialism. On 20th December 1926 Pius XI announced that Mussolini was 'the man sent by Providence' and the corporatist ideas on which Mussolini tried to build his fascist state appeared in a respectable form in the encyclical *Quadragesimo Anno* of 1931. Douglas Hyde has observed that as late as 1951 many Italian bishops were telling him that life had been much better under the fascists.[31] Writing at the end of 1932 Walter Dirks, editor of the Catholic Rhein-Mainische Volkszeitung, expressed the fear that if a Nazi dictatorship were established, the Catholic community would make a similar peace with it as had occurred in Italy. This was in fact what happened. The bishops appreciated and welcomed both the anti-communism of Hitler and his stress on authority and morality. And in his first radio address to the German people after becoming chancellor, Hitler assured them that the members of his government "would preserve and defend those basic principles on which our nation has been built up. They regard Christianity as the foundation of our national morality and the family as the basis of national life".[32]

However beneath this public approval for Christianity lay a deep hatred of its message: 'I promise you that if I wished to, I could destroy the church in a few years; it is hollow and rotten and false through and through. One push and the whole structure would collapse.'[33] In the Nazi Party's indoctrination sessions it was made quite clear that National Socialism and Christianity were incompatible: 'One is either a Nazi or a committed Christian. We affirm *das Volk* as our inheritance and commit ourselves to life. Christianity today affirms *Das Volk* at best as secondary or does it only as an accidental society. For Christianity the true community is that of the faithful.'[34]

It is interesting, incidentally, to compare this statement with the views of John Tyndall of the present-day National Front in Britain. Tyndall refers to the 'fundamental flaw in Christianity': that is, the fact that it seeks to apply love *beyond* the boundaries of nations.[35] Again, in a leaflet issued by the National Front in 1975 we read: 'The church, penetrated throughout by Communists and fellow travellers, no longer cares first and foremost about the spiritual welfare of the

British people, but allies itself with forces of political subversion and violent revolution throughout Britain and the western world.'[36] Another Nazi, speaking at a Party school in 1936, said, 'Christianity and Nazism are like Fire and Water. We must not yet say this openly. Outwardly we must not attack Christianity, we must be far more clever.'[37] So the *public* image was that of Nazi patriotic Christianity. 'True Christianity and True Nazism are identical', said Reich Minister Kerll. 'Since 1933 Hitler has hammered Jesus and his teachings into the hearts of the people.'[38]

The elements within theology which prevented the Church from creating an effective resistance to Nazism, are more complex, and these general comments need to be supplemented by the major studies of J. S. Conway, Richard Gutteridge, and Hans Tiefel.[39] Certainly it is true, as Tiefel says, that in the Lutheran tradition of Germany 'it was assumed that the Christian would stand to the political right, and patriotic religious phrases belonged in every good sermon. German Protestantism after the First World War remained what it had always been . . . conservative and Deutsch National.'[40] Hitler's strong stand against the left was received by most Christians with delight, and they supported these anti-communist measures which, a few years later, were used against the Church.

But, Tiefel argues, there was more to the Lutheran/Nazi alliance than this combination of pietism and nationalism. Lutheran Nazism 'proceeds also on a specific theological/ethical level', based on the duality of law and gospel.[41] Law was pre-Christian and for all men. Gospel was for Christians. So it was possible to know God's will independently of the gospel. There was thus no specific Christian ethic and no Christian social critique. For the gospel spoke of another realm and of another country. The theological defects in Lutheranism made it virtually impossible to develop any social theological critique of Nazism. The point was made powerfully by Paul Tillich in 1936 when he argued that 'it is almost impossible for a nation educated in Lutheranism to proceed from religion to socialism.'[42] Because of Luther's conception of the Kingdom of God as purely transcendent and spiritual, and the harsh division between the Kingdom of God (inward, spiritual, nonpolitical) and the kingdoms of this world (external, material, political), the ground is cut away from Christian social thought. This view was still being stated after the war. So Franz Lau in 1952 could write that 'the Christian, in so far as he is subordinate to the Emperor, has not to pay heed to Christ's law. Christ's law concerns only the sphere of the inward.'[43]

Equally serious was the neglect in German theological circles of the orthodox Christian teaching about the Incarnation, the taking of humanity into God through the taking flesh of the Word. Only Bonhoeffer gave serious attention to the consequences of Christology for social ethics. The world, he argued, was being left to its own devices, while the Church looked to its own affairs: there was a false spirituality rooted in a defective theological tradition.[44] The relationship between Christian orthodoxy and resistance to Hitler remains an important area of study. Certainly there were those in Germany, as in Britain today, who saw the Incarnation as a myth. One such was Gerhard Kittel, Professor of Theology at Tübingen, and an enthusiastic member of the Nazi Party. Kittel supported the exclusion of non-Aryans from the church, the setting up of Jewish ghettoes and Jewish churches, and ruled out pogroms on the grounds of impracticability.[45] It is worth remembering too that Bonhoeffer's *Christology* was written in the year Hitler came to power, and defends the Council of Chalcedon against the theological liberals. Edwin Robertson says in his introduction to the English edition: 'Here in this Christological material is an arsenal from which the Confessing Church would draw many of its weapons to defeat the German Christians and thus prevent the poison of Nazism from destroying the church.'[46]

The British situation today

I want now to ask: are any of the features which I have described present today in our society in Britain? I want to suggest three answers. There is a discernible shift to the right in mainstream politics; this is most noticeable in the Thatcher tendency in the Conservative Party, and the politics of race since the early 1960s show this trend very clearly. The virtual collapse of the older Christian social tradition has deprived the Church of theological resources from which to provide an effective critique of capitalism and emerging fascism. The resurgence of fundamentalism and of pietistic and moral crusading styles of evangelical Christianity, while they have not been explicitly racist or fascist, could easily provide some of the raw material for a new religious fascism.

The resurgence of the right

The shift to the right; it seems hardly necessary to justify this assertion. There are frequent parallels made with the 1930s and, while simplistic comparisons must be avoided, there are clearly points of similarity. Capitalism is again in crisis, the worst crisis since the 1930s. Socialism is weak and divided. The Labour Party is probably absolutely and relatively weaker than at any time since the thirties, and there is widespread disillusionment with all the major parties. Inflation has divided the working-class movement. The traditional British virtues are in doubt. Social problems such as unemployment, lack of decent housing, and inadequate health services provide the raw material for a shift towards authoritarian solutions. There is a growing ideology of repression and surveillance.[47] We have seen the intensifying of racist immigration laws and controls, of repressive legislation in Ireland, the Industrial Relations Act, the use of the conspiracy laws, the extension of police powers, the Misuse of Drugs Act, and so on.[48] We know too that there continue to be high-level discussions about the possible use of para-military groups against organized workers. We have seen the revival of 'reds under the beds' positions and of McCarthyist methods (as in the report *The Attack on Higher Education* from the Institute for the Study of Conflict in 1977 where some 120 individuals were named.)[49] There are many other examples of repressive legislation which, I suggest, contribute to 'creeping fascism'.

Specifically, we have seen in the last two decades a marked shift in both *legislation* and *ideology* over the question of the black population in Britain.[50] Whereas at the end of the 1950s it was only very right-wing Conservatives such as Sir Cyril Osborne who argued for control of immigration, and even he denied any anti-black intentions, by 1978 Mrs Thatcher can openly concede that it is the threat to the British character from other races which is central, and can seek to justify specifically anti-black legislation on the 'number theory of prejudice'.[51] A stage-by-stage comparison of views of mainstream politicians on race, and those of the anti-black and anti-semitic groups from Mosley through to the National Front and British Movement, indicates how, since the late fifties, the pendulum of orthodoxy has moved further to the right. So we find a racist ideology (black people are undesirable *per se*) used to justify racist legislation on immigration *and* anti-racist legislation inside Britain. Yet racism is indivisible, and one cannot promote harmony at the expense of justice.

Mrs Thatcher and the new Tory racism bring one to the background of Thatcher's rise to power, and the influence of such groups as the National Association for Freedom (now the Freedom Association). NAFF, founded in 1975, was linked from its early days with Aims of Industry, which changed its name to Aims for Freedom and Enterprise, and was committed to support for a 'stronger state'. It was founded four weeks after Margaret Thatcher became Tory leader, and Robert Moss, its Director until recently, was a committed Thatcherite. On 9th December 1978 it changed its name to the Freedom Association. Its council includes various counter-insurgency and anti-subversion figures. Its ideological position is anti-welfare state, anti-union, and pro-capitalist, with a Milton Friedman economic line. It stands for 'free choice' in health and education, with the welfare state only for the needy. Politically it is strongly anti-communist, pro-South Africa and Rhodesia, and in favour of increased spending on defence, police, and prisons. Robert Moss, its principal theoretician, in his book *The Collapse of Democracy* (1977) argues for 'civilized intolerance', that is, for intolerance of groups which oppose the constitution. NAFF, and its closely connected groups, Aims for Freedom and Enterprise, and the Institute for the Study of Conflict, are an important element in the shift to the right in the Tory party. The influence of NAFF-type ideas on Margaret Thatcher is considerable, and Robert Moss wrote her 'Iron Maiden' speech. While there is not a fascist ideology here, there is the typical stress on the strong state and an attack on working-class power.[52]

It seems to me, it would be wrong to use the blanket term "fascism" to describe this general rightward shift. What is certainly correct is to recognize that there is this marked trend towards authoritarian rule which, given the right conditions, could lead in the direction of some kind of fascism.[53] For the appeal of classical fascism in its early stages is popular and plausible, and has a great attraction to those decent people who are prepared to exchange justice and freedom for a measure of decency and security. It has a particular appeal for those who feel betrayed by mainstream politics. Many such people can be found among the British churches, and it is this genteel rightism which is a more serious attraction to them than the politics of the National Front. It is interesting too to note the connection between the new Tory right and vaguely church-centred ideas. Mrs Thatcher, along with Lord Hailsham and others, seems to be trying to revive the idea that Conservatism and Christianity are connected. A distinctive "new Christian Right" has emerged, drawing on a number of theological resources within the Christian tradition.[54]

The decay of social theology

Another feature which the British churches share with German churches in the thirties is the absence of any authentic social theology. But there are two crucial differences here. First, whereas Lutheranism was marked from the outset by an other-worldly theology, Anglicanism has a long and venerable tradition of social and socialist thought. Yet it is this tradition which, with certain hopeful and striking exceptions, is now in decay. So we are talking not of a *lack* of social theology but of its *collapse*. The second difference is that the British churches today are, by any standards, far more aware of the links between theology and social responsibility than were the German churches of the thirties. The record of the churches in Britain on racism is certainly better than that of many other groupings. So, as in the social and economic parallels, the theological parallels should not be overplayed.

Nevertheless there are lessons from the thirties which we can usefully learn. In 1940 Reinhold Niebuhr pointed to the theological rationale of the strong state.

> It is perhaps not too much to say that Germany finds herself in her present plight because the theology of the Lutheran Reformation which informed her religious life discouraged any great interest in the problem of justice. It simply took for granted that men are evil, and asserted that a strong state is required to hold their sins in check.[55]

Today the prevailing trends in British theology are also hostile to serious social theology but for quite different reasons. At the sophisticated level we have the 'establishment theology' of many 'radical' theologians, which seems to be marked by a kind of historical relativism combining radicalism in theology with extreme conservatism in social attitudes. Mascall has commented:

> Not the least weakness of this type of radical secularization is that it entirely undermines the whole notion of Christian social theology: just because it completely capitulates to the outlook of the contemporary world, it has no criteria for passing judgement on it.[56]

In the writings of many mainstream British theologians, one sees a theology with no political consequences apart from that of reinforcing the *status quo* by default. Theology becomes a human construction, relative and subject to change; it ceases to present any challenge to secular structures. So theological relativism tends to lead to secular conformity. At the level of popular Christianity, the seventies have seen a good deal of 'instant social comment', typified by Archbishop Coggan's 'Call to the Nation' of 1975 where cliché and platitude replaced serious theological analysis. Christian social theology sees the role of theologians to involve critical relationship to secular structures. But much of today's western theology functions in isolation from the world.[57]

The revival of fundamentalism and intolerance

In addition to the adaptation of much theology to secular trends we see also the resurgence of that type of fundamentalism which tends to lead to a reactionary political position. Of course, it is important to recognize that modern evangelicalism is a multi-faceted phenomenon. One of the most encouraging features of present-day Christianity is the growth of an evangelical social voice, and while this is most evident in the USA and in Third World countries, its presence in Britain has not been insignificant.[58] Nevertheless the spread of an irrational and intolerant fundamentalism remains a very disturbing facet of recent Christian history. Dominated by a stress on law and order, rooted in a rigid literalism of biblical interpretation, and attracting to its support many individuals of marked authoritarian outlook, its potential for harm is very great. The history of fundamentalism gives little hope for believing that it can ever live happily with social radicalism, and the recent history of fundamentalist movements of social protest reinforces one's worst fears.

It is against this background that one must view a movement which has developed in Britain during the 1970s, the Nationwide Festival of Light. It is significant that few, if any, church leaders have publicly criticized the positions and attitudes of this body, though there is some evidence that the popularity and uncritical support which it for a time attracted may be on the wane. In 1972 I drew attention to the grave danger that the Festival of Light could become an umbrella movement for the evangelical ultra-right,[59] though I also then felt that perhaps as a movement, it was too simplistic to present a serious danger to Christianity, however much it might make Christians appear ridiculous.[60] I think that assessment was over-optimistic, and did not take enough account of the disturbing growth of irrationalism and intolerance among the more reactionary types of evangelical, as well as among the very threatened middle class. I believe that, however slight its influence may be, the Festival of Light tendency does represent an extremely harmful type of Christianity, based on a crude fundamentalism which is very similar to that which I described earlier in a different context. Linked with this is the same kind of irrationalism and fanaticism. The social position of the movement is best represented in the writings of its Director, O. R. Johnston, whose central theme is the corruption of culture.[61] Johnston combines a crude fundamentalism with a high degree of very generalized social comment and a certainty that the Festival of Light is God's instrument to achieve social righteousness.

The movement of social and moral protest spearheaded by Mary Whitehouse is in some crucial respects different from the Festival of Light. Although Mrs Whitehouse appears to be a Christian in some sense, the theological element in her movement is less clear and seems to be limited to a personal belief in God and in Jesus Christ, and a devotion of an affective-pietistic type. But one finds in Mary Whitehouse the same kind of bigoted intolerance and the same use of sweeping generalizations which one finds in the Festival, though Mrs Whitehouse is perhaps more prone to abuse, rudeness, and the smear technique.[62] It is important in considering the Whitehouse movement to realize that her pedigree is that of Moral Rearmament, and the style of her writing and approach will be familiar to those with past acquaintance with MRA. Mary Whitehouse joined the Oxford Group in 1935,[63] and, while her involvement in MRA is not clear, the MRA ethos and technique is only too evident. The history of MRA was studied closely by the late Tom Driberg, who made much of the alleged statement by its founder, Frank Buchman:

> I thank heaven for a man like Adolf Hitler who built a front line of defence against the Anti-Christ of Communism . . . But think what it would mean if Hitler surrendered to the control of God. Or Mussolini. Or any dictator. Through such a man God could control a nation overnight and solve every last bewildering problem.[64]

In his reply to an earlier pamphlet by Driberg, Canon J. P. Thornton-Duesbury quotes other statements indicating an anti-Nazi position.[65] But the point is that movements of the MRA type, with their simplistic anti-Communism combined with an irrational form of Christian pietism, are very vulnerable to becoming stooges of the ultra-right, and the historical data show that this has in fact happened.

In fact, Hitler's own posture as a moral reformer and crusader did attract to the Nazi movement many of those good and sincere people who were concerned with the corruption of culture. But soon Hitler's concern with moral purity was taken up by the evangelical anti-Semites in the United States.

In 1933 the Revd Gerald B. Winrod of Kansas formed an organization called the Defenders of the Christian Faith. After a visit to Germany in that year, Winrod became openly pro-Nazi. His movement saw the Jews as 'contaminators in the moral realm'.

> One of the first things that disgusted Hitler was that he discovered that centers of vice, nudist colonies, the filthy screen and stage as well as the poison of literature to be *under control and direction of an organization of Jews*, who for money were willing to tear down the Gentile morals of the nation. the women saw the tide of mass immorality sweeping their country and organized to give defiant opposition to every form of unbridled lust about the time Adolf Hitler appeared on the scene making a dynamic appeal to popular imagination. By degrees he won the confidence of the women and succeeded in enlisting their support behind his movement. They came to him like an avalanche because his political philosophy provided for the upbuilding of the moral standards of the nation.[66]

Now of course there is no certainty that, simply because moral crusades in the past have often moved towards the reactionary right, all such movements will tend to do the same. Movements such as the Festival of Light and other similar crusading groups are not explicitly right-wing, although they show little evidence of sympathy with socialism! However, they do seem to possess precisely those features which, *given the right conditions*, could lead them in the direction of some kind of fascism: a crude fundamentalist theology, a following of highly vulnerable, very threatened, middle-class and particularly suburban people – the very group from which Hitler derived his mass support – and a leadership marked by intolerance, irrational polemic, and absolute conviction that they are right. The comparison which is often made between such movements and other disturbing groups such as the National Front is by no means far-fetched, and scrutiny of the publications of the National Front and other racist groups discovers a strong emphasis on the 'moral purity' issue.[67] It is necessary, to avoid misunderstanding, however, to re-emphasize the nature of the argument. One is not claiming that there is a close comparison to be drawn, in terms of intention and fundamental belief, between groups of sincere (if, as we believe, mistaken) Christians, and groups of organized racists of the National Front type: but simply that, in the right conditions, the same people may be attracted to both, and that a movement which begins with a sincere and Christian aim may find itself led into harmful and evil paths.

Summary

To summarize, I believe that we are moving into a more repressive and intolerant society, that we are in a process of 'creeping fascism'. Within this context, the resurgence of fundamentalism and of religious fanaticism is potentially extremely dangerous. Unless we see a reversal of the other-worldly trends in much current theology, and a renewal of Christian prophecy, it is certain that this dangerous phenomenon will increase. It is not 'Christian Fascism' so much as a defective theology which can easily aid the growth of fascism and become part of its ideological apparatus. Most of the Christians who fell for the Hitler movement were not particularly wicked or even particularly racist. Hitler himself did not assume an explicitly anti-Christian mantle in public: on the contrary he was the representative of true Christianity. His appeal, for moral order and defence against the communist peril, is still one which is likely to evoke a response from many good Christians. Before they respond, they need to reconsider the lessons of history.

11
The Local Roots of Fascism

The danger of fascism

Fascism as was argued earlier is not merely racism, racial violence, authoritarianism, repression, increased police powers, or any form of dictatorship. All these features may be elements in a process of 'creeping fascism', but fascism is more than them all. Fascism is one possible development from capitalist society when it has reached a certain stage and if it does not move towards socialism. Fascism is not therefore a plot or a conspiracy; it is a logical result of certain processes of development. It is a phenomenon of industrial society in severe socio-economic crisis, confronted on the one hand with the threat of collapse, and on the other with the threat of socialism. And those who are most threatened by the attraction and appeal of fascism are not the poor, but rather the powerful whose vested interests of wealth and power are threatened by the possibility of social change, and the suburban middle class for whom the early stages of growth of a fascist movement may appear highly reputable, moral, and even Christian. Hitler's early campaign had the feel of a moral crusade, and it was certainly very appealing to those Christians who were willing to exchange justice and freedom for a measure of decency and security. Today the danger of fascism comes far more from these groups, and the movements created to defend their interests, than it does from the National Front and other grass-roots racist groups.[1]

It is therefore in the powerful regions of the city, and in the suburbs that the danger of a new fascism is most serious. For it is where power and privilege are most concentrated that there will be most resistance to change. However, the urban poor may well be drawn to fascism as a means of solving their problems, and it is here, in the decayed districts, that the openly racist groups are particularly active and most vicious.

But their presence in these districts is not new, and is simply the latest manifestation of the sense of paralysis and powerlessness in these districts. To concentrate merely on resisting and opposing the National Front on the streets of Bethnal Green, Lewisham, and Manchester, important as this is, may be to miss the far greater danger of respectable, gentrified fascism in the corridors of power.

Fascist movements in the East End of London

Nevertheless the inner city districts are of vital importance. I want here to describe the growth of racist and fascist groups in one area, the East End of London. In the days of the large-scale immigration of Ashkenazi Jews from Eastern Europe, there was a great deal of organized anti-Semitic propaganda in the East End, associated particularly with such names as Arnold White and Major Evans-Gordon.[2] These new Jewish immigrants were blamed even by the descendants of the Irish immigrants of the 1840s for the same evils for which their own parents had been blamed earlier: while in the 1840s the descendants of the Huguenots had blamed the Irish. Today it is not unknown for some East End Jews to blame the Bengalis, who now inhabit the old Jewish streets in Whitechapel, for the bad conditions in the district. There are in fact very close parallels between the arguments and the language used against the Jews at the turn of the century and those used against the Asians in the 1970s.[3] Similarly, the campaign for control of immigration shows a depressingly similar pattern in both periods.[4]

In the 1950s J. H. Robb[5] showed the central place played by Bethnal Green in the formation of anti-immigrant feeling. For Bethnal Green, adjacent to the Jewish ghetto in Whitechapel, was still, in the first few decades of this century, a largely white district, populated by people who had been born locally. The sense of being threatened by the alien presence to the south was easy to exploit and to transform into active anti-Semitism. So after 1902, and particularly in the 1930s, many racist and fascist groups were active in the East End: the British Empire Union (1919), The Britons (1918), the National Citizens' Union (1919), the British Fascisti (1923), the British National Fascists (1924), the Imperial Fascism League (1929), Mosley's British Union of Fascists (1932), and the National Socialist League (1937) – to name only the main ones. During 1936 East London police attended 536 meetings in August, 603 in September, and 647 in October. The British Union of Fascists claimed 4,000 members in Bethnal Green at this period. In 1937 the BUF contested Bethnal Green South West and Shoreditch and in Bethnal Green they polled over 3,000 votes. Later in 1937 every ward in Bethnal Green was contested.[6] The districts of Bethnal Green and Shoreditch are still, forty years later, the focal points for fascist activity in the East End. The National Front and the British Movement have been able to draw not only on the sense of powerlessness in the districts but also on this long tradition of fascism and anti-Semitism. Moreover these two districts, Bethnal Green and Shoreditch, are districts of relatively low mobility, containing many families who have been there for many generations, and where folk memories are long.

In the 1950s a new wave of anti-immigrant polemic in the East End focused upon the decayed district of Cable Street near the London Docks. This district, west of Cannon Street Road, had, during and after the Second World War, become a social centre for merchant seamen from West, East, and North Africa, and later from the Caribbean and Asia.[7] Some black people had been around the Cable Street area for many years, and one Arab café in Leman Street dated back to just after the First World War. The western end of Cable Street had become a café quarter and was also a centre of prostitution. The racist groups focused their attack on prostitution and bad housing. In 1945 the Communist MP for Mile End, Phil Piratin, was warning of the revival of Mosleyite activity, and a meeting of Stepney Communist Party on 12 October 1947 referred to 'the revival of Fascist activity in the East End'.[8] The story is therefore not a new one, and there is a continuous tradition of anti-immigrant polemic which goes back many years. On 29 May 1958 an East London branch of the National Labour Party – John Bean's movement which later merged with the White Defence League of Colin Jordan to form the British National Party (1960) – was formed in

Bethnal Green, at a pub in Cheshire Street, near to Brick Lane.[9] The NLP decided to launch an intensive campaign in the area, and this was continued and intensified after the creation of the BNP two years later. Meetings were held regularly at the junction of Cheshire Street and St Matthew's Row, a site which on Sundays was part of Brick Lane street market. This site had been used by the Mosleyites, and in the 1979 General Election campaign, Martin Webster of the National Front used the same site. The BNP's paper *Combat* regularly featured the East End. So, once again, Bethnal Green, with its largely white population, was the base for an attack on Whitechapel, not far to the south, with large numbers of immigrants. 'Stepney vice is a black problem', announced *Combat* in 1961. 'It has been left to the British National Party speakers at their regular Sunday meetings in nearby Bethnal Green to denounce this blot on the face of East London'.[10] So local fears and resentments were aroused, and the presence of a small criminal community among the West African and Maltese immigrants was used as the basis for an attack on all immigrants. But behind this activity and the support it aroused lay years of resentment at the neglect of the needs of all the population. It is this resentment and frustration which provides the raw material for the racist activity today.

At the end of the 1950s there was more Mosleyite activity. In 1953 a Union Movement candidate in the LCC election in Stepney gained 10 per cent of the poll, getting twice the number of votes of the local Tory candidate: but the total number of votes for the UM candidate was only 64, an indication of the general state of apathy. There were violent scenes in Dalston in 1962, and four years later Mosley stood as parliamentary candidate for Shoreditch. It is against this background of a persisting tradition of working-class white support for Mosley and his successors that the recent revival of fascist activity in these same areas is to be seen.

The National Front

After the National Front was created, out of a fusion of three rather different groups on the ultra-right, in 1967, there was not a great deal of evidence of significant support in the East End, or indeed anywhere else, for some years. The entry into the race debate of Enoch Powell, with his 'rivers of blood' speech of 1968, helped to deflect support from the National Front for some time. But after 1972, when there was some movement from the right wing of the Tory Party into the Front, and particularly after 1974, the Front began to make important progress, and the East End became the focus for their London activities. In the General Election of October 1974, the National Front candidates obtained 7.6 per cent of the poll in Bethnal Green and Bow, and 9.4 per cent in Shoreditch and Hackney South, the highest ratio in the whole of Britain.[11] On 6 September 1975, the Front held its first major march through the East End, an anti-mugging march. It was not a great success in statistical terms – some 680 people from all over the country – but it was a symbolic opening for their evil campaign in the area. In the GLC elections of May 1977 they pushed the liberals into fourth place.[12]

Between 1976 and 1978 the activities of the National Front increased in the East End. A regular distribution point for their racist and inflammatory literature was established in Bethnal Green Road, and National Front members gathered there each Sunday morning. A nearby pub became their unofficial headquarters, and the local Asian community in Brick Lane became the prime target of their hostility. On the night of the local elections in May 1978 Altab Ali was murdered, and, while there was no clear evidence of direct links with the National Front activity, it was difficult to isolate the incident from the sustained and intensive campaign of racial hatred which had been organized in the Brick Lane area. Certainly the Asian community, who organized a symbolic carrying of a coffin to Downing Street on 14 May 1978, saw this as a racist murder. Within a month, there was another murder, a few miles north in Hackney. And on 11 June some 150 white youths rampaged through Brick Lane in a violent escapade, which many informed observers believed to have been organized by local racists. In the following months there was increased evidence of attacks on Asians in the area.[13]

At the May 1978 elections, the National Front did less well in the area as a whole. The anti-racist movements had organized a very successful Carnival Against the Nazis which had gathered some 80,000 people to march from Trafalgar Square to Victoria Park in Bethnal Green, and the success of this carnival had done much to undermine the credibility of the National Front. In Shoreditch and Hackney South the over-all vote for the Front was down from 19 per cent in the GLC elections of 1977 to 16.8 per cent, while in Bethnal Green and Bow it was down from 19 to 10 per cent. Even so, some wards showed high ratios for the NF candidates – 23 per cent in St Peter's Ward, Bethnal Green, where anti-immigrant activity had focused around a new GLC estate, and 25 per cent in the Moorfields Ward adjoining Hoxton.

In the same period, there was a marked increase in slogans on walls and bridges in the area, announcing support for the National Front, and advocating anti-black attitudes. A local campaign to remove such racist slogans met with opposition from the police who insisted that to remove slogans would constitute an offence, although in December 1977 the magistrate at Old Street dismissed a case against five local trade unionists who had removed slogans from a railway bridge, and told them that they had improved the state of the bridge by doing so.[14] More serious than the slogans, however, was the undoubted relationship between the National Front activity and the incidence of attacks on Asians in the area, which was well documented in a report from the local trades council.[15]

After the carnival in 1978 the success of the National Front in the East End began to wane. They had failed to attract a mass following of young people, many of whom had turned to the Anti-Nazi League side because they had managed to harness the best rock bands such as Tom Robinson Band and Steel Pulse. By comparison, the hundred or so 'Young NF' supporters who heckled the carnival seemed a somewhat pathetic and miserable fringe group. Also the increased involvement of black teenagers in sport, particularly in boxing, had helped to turn the tables against the Front. It was these fairly ordinary day-to-day 'apolitical' factors which probably did more than the more cerebral attacks on the NF ideology to reduce their popularity in the East End. At the same time, the activity of local anti-racist organizations was important, and the constant reiteration of the Nazi origins of the Front certainly was an essential element in bringing about their decline. In July 1978 Frank Berry, former chairman of the local branch of the National Front, resigned after ten years, claiming that the National Front constituted 'a danger to the community'.[16] By the time of the General Election of 1979, Mrs Thatcher had managed to steal a good deal of the racist vote from the National Front, and, although they had put up their 'heavy battalions' (Tyndall in Shoreditch and Hackney South, and Webster in Bethnal Green and Bow) in the East End, they did less well than their relatively unknown candidates in the previous election.[17] The Tory vote went up, and Mrs Thatcher's exploitation of anti-immigrant feeling since her January 1978 speech on television was successful. Since then, the National Front has been torn apart by internal dissensions, leading to the formation of a new party, the British People's Party, and, while there have been frantic attempts, as at Southwark on 2 March 1980, to rally the forces together, it seems likely that the party will decline more as the years go by. Yet it is also likely that it will continue to exercise a harmful effect in such districts as the East End, an effect which will be as out of proportion to its size, as has been the case in the history of its antecedent bodies.

The support for the National Front in the East End has come from working-class people and particularly from the disillusioned youth. One of the myths of fascist historiography is that support for fascist movements comes exclusively from the *petite bourgeoisie.* This was not true in Hitler's Germany and it is not true in Britain today, though it is certainly the case that the suburban middle class does represent the strongest section of the public attracted by the appeal of fascism. In terms of membership, the largest single section of the National Front seems to come from manual workers, although, in relation to their size, the archaic classes are disproportionately represented in the movement. At the same time, it would be quite mistaken to view the National Front, as Martin Walker appears to do in his study, as a middle-class backlash movement.[18] The work at Essex University by Harrap and Zimmerman suggests that NF votes come mainly from young, working-class and poorly educated people.[19]

National Front candidates showed a higher proportion of manual workers than the other two parties: one third of the NF candidates studied by Harrap and Zimmerman were manual workers compared with 1 in 15 candidates for the Labour Party. On this evidence, the National Front had more basis to claim to be a working-class party than had either the Labour or Communist Parties.[20]

John Tyndall, the former National Front leader, made much of the claim that the appeal of the NF was to working-class people. 'The National Front', he claimed, 'in fact recruits an enormous portion of its members from the so-called "working class" . . . '[21] And in fact the voting support for the Front has been concentrated in working-class areas. In the East End, the appeal seemed to be particularly successful among those disillusioned with the Labour Party record, and among the alienated youth. Earlier, Mosley had claimed, in reference to the 1930s, that 'if the young had then had the vote, we should have won easily.'[22] In 1978 a British study of the young NF supporter, based in Hoxton, showed that, out of 301 young whites aged 16–20 who were interviewed, 13 per cent said that the National Front was their first-choice party.[23] The group of people most strongly committed to the Front was the young, male, unskilled, who had left school at 16 without qualifications. The survey however distinguished between the committed and the sympathetic: while the committed fascist was more likely to come from the middle-class and white-collar sector, there was a wide area of sympathy among the young working class and particularly among the disillusioned and the marginalized. For many of the young NF supporters who rampaged through Brick Lane on Sundays in 1978, the subtleties of fascism as outlined in *Spearhead* were of no interest. The NF had given respectability in their minds to 'Paki-bashing' and to race hatred. More than that, it had given these very disturbed and frustrated adolescents an identity for the first time.

In gathering support for the National Front, the race issue was central. In 1975 there was a split in the NF which centred largely on the issue of how the party could maintain its working-class support. The 'populists' wanted to discuss a wide range of issues apart from race. In *Spearhead* for July

1975, Martin Webster compared results in two local elections. In one, the NF had tried to broaden the issues and 'produced an election address which only mentioned Coloured Immigration once, in small print . . .' The party did badly. In the other, the campaign focused solely on the question of the blacks, and did much better. Webster commented:

> If the British people are destroyed through racial interbreeding, then the British nation will cease to exist. If we cannot get *that* message through to the British people, then *all* of our other policies, no matter how important they are in themselves, will be utterly meaningless and irrelevant.[24]

Two years earlier, John Tyndall had also stressed the importance of the massive demonstration in arousing support among working-class people.

> What is it that touches off a chord in the instincts of the people to whom we seek to appeal? It can often be the most simple and primitive thing. Rather than a speech or printed article it may be just a flag; it may be a marching column; it may be the sound of a drum; it may be a banner or it may just be the impression of a crowd. None of these things contain in themselves one single argument, one single piece of logic . . . They are recognized as being among the things that appeal to the hidden forces in the human soul.[25]

The spectacular march is therefore an essential part of the NF campaign.

The struggle against fascism

One reason, of course, why the National Front has been popular in the East End has been the fact that there has been no tradition of voting Tory. On the other hand, the Labour Party includes a wide range of political outlooks, including some very right-wing positions. The attitudes on race taken up by the National Front may be in essence no different from those adopted and expressed, in more genteel language, by many Tory and Labour spokesmen at local level in many areas. Again, in the East End there is a widespread sense of frustration with the Labour establishment so that many working-class people have voted for the National Front purely out of despair. An article in the *Observer* in 1977 noted:

> The people of Hoxton feel betrayed, even conspired against by the Labour Party, who have taken their votes for granted for many years. They would rather lose their right arms than vote Tory, but they will, and they do, vote for the National Front – often out of pure spite. 'The *candidate* doesn't matter', said an NF election organizer. 'You could put up the devil himself in Hoxton.'[26]

The appeal of the NF in a working-class district is often attractive for, unlike many of the left-wing groups which are organized and dominated by middle-class and 'student-class' people with private means, the NF is seen to be a working-class party with roots in the local community. The contrast with some of the well-known 'Marxist' groups could not be more glaring. Here there are often virtually no roots in the working-class community, and virtually no workers among the leadership. To many people in the East End, the Marxist groups seem to be simply the latest wave of middle-class do-gooders who have come from elsewhere. They are treated with contempt. As many Bethnal Green people have commented, 'We have to go on living here when they have gone through.' On the other hand, many NF supporters do live in the East End and are well established there. And where the groups on the left have also established roots and worked with and within the local community, the support has noticeably increased: examples are the very popular campaign of the Communist Solly Kaye in Stepney in the 1950s – his graffiti are still extant on walls in the area – and the Socialist Unity campaign in Spitalfields in 1978.

The most important feature of the East End fascist activity is that it has focused on generations of neglect of basic social needs: poor schools, bad health care delivery, overcrowding, unemployment, and so on. Most of all, there is the sense of being out of contact with the sources of power and the instruments of change. Thus there grows up a dangerous form of social autism, an inability to effect change. So vandalism becomes the last available form of social action. In one sense, the rise of the National Front and the British Movement represents vandalism expanded into a political ideology.

If the local base of fascism is to be destroyed, there needs to be local action in the deprived and neglected areas which are the breeding grounds for fascist activity. Often anti-fascists appear in these districts to be merely idealists or political activists who are there for a season, but are uninvolved in the real, day-to-day lives and struggles of the people, and who simply do not understand. Sometimes, however, the fascists do at least seem to understand their plight. To be a professional anti-fascist, moving on the circuit from demo to demo, is to play into the hands of the fascist groups, unless there goes along with this a deeper commitment at the local level. There needs to be a deep involvement in such issues as health care, tenants' rights, the care of the old and lonely, the unemployed, the disenchanted youth, the groups who are most vulnerable to simplistic explanations. Fascism cannot be defeated from a safe distance by people who are remote from the problems which it highlights.

Out of the East End's experience and reaction to its own social history and its immigrants have come both racism and radicalism. They provided a microcosm of the options for British society.

12 *Theological Renewal and the Catholic Left*

The church in a right-wing era

The current political situation has been described as one of 'global Rightism'. In the UK we have seen the growth of 'Thatcherism', the new ideology of the Tory Party, a backward-looking phenomenon, which asserts traditional ideological values and themes such as family, nation, patriotism, free enterprise, authority, and law and order. 'The Great Moving Right Show' is on.[1] What we are witnessing is a type of authoritarian populism, similar to classical fascism, but retaining most of the formal representative institutions. The movement attacks welfare scroungers, subversives, permissives. In some forms of the syndrome, the alien threat becomes a racial threat: it is black people who threaten the *moral* order. In other forms, the enemy may be homosexuals, liberals, trade unionists, Marxists. Such words as these might be used to alert the public to the threat of anarchy:

> The streets of our country are in turmoil. The universities are filled with students rebelling and rioting. Communists are seeking to destroy our country. Russia is threatening us with her might and the republic is in danger. Yes, danger from within and without. We need law and order. Without it our nation cannot survive.

Unfortunately, however, those words come from the lips of Adolf Hitler, speaking in 1932. They remain as a powerful warning to us.

In this situation, there is a twofold danger for the Church. It may be tempted to give some kind of religious sanction to the shift to the right. The era of Archbishop Coggan illustrates the way in which a simplistic moralism may help to provide such sanction. Or, secondly, the Church may withdraw into a false spirituality, a concern with the 'inner soul of man' and with the 'ethereal qualities of immortality', a concern which received enthusiastic support in the 1978 Reith Lectures by Dr E. R. Norman.[2] However, the Church may seek a third way: it may seek to exercise a prophetic role. But this may collapse for lack of adequate theological and spiritual roots. If this third option is in fact the correct one, and the Church is called to a renewal of its critical prophetic role, then it follows that it is also called to a return to a theological tradition in which contemplative prayer and political consciousness are united. Dom Helder Camara has suggested that we need theologians who will do with Marx what Thomas Aquinas did with Aristotle,[3] while Jon Sobrino and others have stressed the need for a liberation spirituality.[4] It is possible that we are on the verge of a new shift in Christian consciousness, a shift towards a new synthesis of the mystical and the political. I want to suggest that the only way in which this shift can occur is by the recovery of orthodoxy.

The renewal of theology

The theological renewal which is called for includes a renewal in theological method, as the Latin American writers have told us. One cannot renew a distortion. But here I wish to draw attention to the direction, the inner thrust, of theology. In his important, if rather polemical study, *The Freedom of Man*, Paul Verghese[5] speaks of five distortions, pathological features, of western theology, and these will serve as a basis for our examination. I shall take Verghese's five points and expand on them in discussing the theological trends of the last few decades.

(i) *A low view of the Incarnation, and the collapse of a genuine Christian mysticism*. In orthodoxy, all theology is mystical theology[6], and is rooted in the Incarnation. However, in recent British 'radical theology' of *The Myth of God Incarnate* type we find the view that the Incarnation is incredible to modern man and must therefore be revised.[7] There needs to be a 're-making of Christian doctrine' so that modern man can believe again. The result of this theological trend is a disturbing kind of cultural conformism. Or the Incarnation may appear, as in the lectures of E. R. Norman, simply as a memory, a reminder that once 'the visible and unseen worlds were briefly joined.'[8] Against this, orthodox theology has insisted that the purpose of the Incarnation was the raising of humanity to share the life of God, and this is the basis of Christian mysticism. In the words of St Gregory Nazianzen: 'For that which he has not assumed he has not healed. . . If the whole of his (Adam's) nature fell, it must be united to the whole nature of him who is begotten, and so saved in the whole.'

Don Cupitt has argued that orthodox Christology was modelled on the Emperor cult. So the elevated Jesus, the 'Christ of Christendom', reinforces monarchy and repression. He cites the words of Eusebius: 'Because there is one God, there is one sovereign.' So monotheism and monarchy go together. But this is to confuse Constantine with Chalcedon, for this is the Constantinian Christ, not the Chalcedonian Christ. Trinitarian orthodoxy is not monotheism of this type, but rather stresses that there is a life of equality and sharing within the Godhead. So a well-known English priest could, on the basis of this creed, put these words on his church notice board: 'As in the Holy Trinity, so in this parish: None is before or after other, none is greater or less than another.' The Incarnation has revolutionary consequences for our social thinking.

(ii) *A flight from the world and the collapse of Christian materialism*. So Christianity comes to be linked with idealism against realism and materialism. (It is this assumption of the idealist character of Christian thought which leads to the view that Christianity is *essentially* opposed to Marxism.) Two examples of this flight from the world are the growth of false spirituality and the resurgence of millenarianism. In spite of its many good and beneficial facets, the spread of the charismatic movement does seem frequently to represent the false spirituality which has so often tied Christianity down to a Neoplatonist or idealist view of reality. In his early study of campus Pentecostalism over ten years ago, Henri Nouwen commented that theologically this movement did seem to be a step backwards from the more wholesome world-embracing theology of the Second Vatican Council.[9] There seems now to be a good deal of charismatic unreality about in the United States and Britain. The resurgence of millenarianism is another form of by-passing social reality, for it pushes all concern with the transformation of the material world into the millenial age. A good example of this Christian futurism is the amazing success of Hal Lindsey's book *The Late Great Planet Earth*.

The result of these trends in Christian thought is other-worldliness and anti-materialism. The essential materialism of orthodox Christian theology gives way to E. R. Norman's concern with the 'ethereal qualities of immortality'. Norman even speaks of the new birth of water and the spirit as 'that most ethereal of images'[10] The use of ether as an element in Christian theology is interesting. Marx, of course, saw religion as an opiate, and to introduce ether into the discussion is at least an original way of dissociating oneself from Marxist categories! But it should be remembered that ether is also a drug of addiction, and ether addiction in fact became endemic in Ulster in the nineteenth century (as Dr Norman might know, since he has also written a history of Ireland). Ether abuse spread as a reaction against the anti-alcohol campaign of one Father Matthew, and at one point there were estimated to be some 50,000 ether addicts in Cookstown.[11] It is perhaps equally true to see the present false spirituality as a similar reaction against the often superficial radicalism of the 1960s. Yet in the New Testament nothing could be less ethereal than the Kingdom of God. Moreover, the discontinuity between the Kingdom of God and this world is not chronological or ecclesiastical, but is to do with the *ordering* of the world.

It is worth noting, in passing, that there is a certain parallel in developments within contemporary Marxism and in the criticisms of the alleged inadequacy of Marxism by some Left critics. One can identify a kind of 'false spirituality' among modern pseudo-Marxist academics which separates theory and consciousness from the material realities of the world.[12] The stress, among some feminist critics of Marxism, on changing consciousness rather than industrial organization seems somewhat reminiscent of Christian theological debates.[13] Yet over twenty years ago John Lewis, looking at the Church through Marxist eyes, drew attention to three factors which helped to perpetuate its false spirituality: the attack on reason and science, a theological anti-rationalism; 'mysticism' (his term for pietism); and the doctrine of total depravity. These three elements he saw as philosophies of counter-revolution.[14] The parallels with the present seem close.

(iii) *A low view of humanity and the collapse of Christian humanism.* In much western Christianity, under the influence of the Augustinian tradition, human beings are seen as totally corrupt and depraved, and nature and grace are violently opposed. Thus the widespread division between what is 'natural' and what is 'Christian' as if Christianity demanded the rejection of nature. Yet the abolition of the 'two planes' theology of natural and supernatural was perhaps the greatest theological achievement of the Second Vatican Council, and the major work of Karl Rahner was a careful and important preparation for this. *Gaudium et Spes* stressed that the effects of grace in Christians are the same as the effects in all human beings.[15] Segundo, following Gutierrez, has rightly stressed that a theology of human liberation could only have arisen on the basis of this major theological revolution.[16] Yet the view of the nature/grace relationship which appears in Rahner and in the Vatican texts is quite different from that which emerges in much earlier Western theology. Reinhold Niebuhr, for example, seems to see the practice of Christian love as virtually impossible in the fallen world because of incompatible interests.[17] His theology is ultimately a theology of hopelessness, a theological form of Karl Popper's 'social engineering': the most one can hope to achieve is a balance of interests, even a balance of terror.

Now an earlier generation of Anglican socialists saw the Christian hope and the human struggle for liberation as a unity. Thus Conrad Noel, writing of the Catholic Crusade in 1933:[18]

> It is necessary for the beginner to grasp this conviction about the nature of God and of Man if he is to understand our idea of sacraments, of authority, of civil government, of politics and economics. The Catholic Crusade philosophy is all of a piece. It will change your views on music, on decoration, on the colour of a piece of material, equally with your views of man's end, the reading of history and the revolution.

Noel was a Christian humanist who did not oppose nature and grace. Christ was really present not only in the sacrament but also in the personalities of splendid men and women made in God's image.[19] And in this view, he was well within the tradition of the Eastern fathers. St Irenaeus stressed that it was man, not merely part of man, which was made in the image of God. The Eastern view of the glory of man comes out strongly in these beautiful words from Gregory of Nyssa: 'You alone are a similitude of Eternal Beauty: and if you look at him, you will become what he is, imitating him who shines within you.'[20] That is a very different view of human nature from the gloomy pessimism of much Western religion. Yet it is more true to orthodoxy with its stress on the glory of man, on 'the image we possess *by nature*' (St Symeon the New Theologian).

At the heart of this low view of human nature is the place of sin. In contrast to the Augustinian understanding that sin is natural to man, the Eastern theologians are emphatic that 'sin does not belong to human nature, but is a parasitic and abnormal growth.'[21] The division about what is natural to the human condition is of the greatest importance theologically, not least in developing the Christian critique of fascism. For in the thought of Nietzsche, which was to influence the ideology of Nazism, Christianity and its values undermined manliness. What was natural to man was repudiated by the demands of the gospel. Conversely, fascism, today as yesterday, exalts and glorifies those tendencies in man which in fact man must transcend in order to be fully human.[22] It is therefore of the greatest urgency that we devote attention to the renewal of what Pope John Paul II in *Redemptor Hominis* has called 'authentic humanism'.[23] Again, it is worth noting the parallel with Marxism where the quest for a socialist humanism has been a central feature of the Marxist world since the late fifties.

In a recent study Gregory Baum stresses the need to see the connection between the possibility of human transformation and that of the transformation of society, and he argues against the use of a doctrine of total depravity to produce a kind of social autism, an inability to effect change.

> The biblical faith understood in the Catholic tradition has always included the conviction that the grace of God *truly*

> *transforms* human life. God's redemption brings creation marred by sin to the fulfilment of its own inclination. In traditional Scholastic language 'grace perfects nature'. Against the Reformers' emphasis on the abiding sinfulness of life, the Council of Trent insisted that the sanctification produced by divine grace was an actual transformation of the human being.

Yet this theology of transformation has been mainly applied to the personal life. It is important now, claims Baum, to apply it to the social dimensions of human struggle, and it is here that the doctrine of total depravity can be a serious obstacle. Baum goes on:

> Let me also present a theological argument against the doctrine of total depravity, applied to a culture or a nation. According to the Catholic tradition, at least, wherever people struggle for their self-understanding and co-operate in the creation of a representative culture, the mystery of God is present to them. God's victory in Jesus Christ assured the universality of divine grace. There is no culture from which God is wholly absent. A purely demonic enterprise can not endure for long. The Nazi reign only lasted twelve years. Present in the culture of any people are the dream of the promised land and the yearning for the peaceful community. There are hints of sacramentality in the experience of any nation. In my view it is the task of critical theology to discover these hints.[24]

(iv) *An individualistic view of salvation and the collapse of the Christian social tradition*. The individualistic understanding of the gospel is not peculiar to the evangelical tradition, though it is still most pronounced there. Thus a well-known evangelical writer observes: 'While emphasizing that there is a distinctive biblical worldview and while inculcating the more general implications of the Gospel with regard to society, his primary concern is with the individual's experience of the saving work of Christ in his own life.'[25] This individualism persists in much of the 'social concern' of the charismatic renewal. Thus Larry Christensen's book *A Charismatic Approach to Social Action*[26] takes a low view of the political world. The Church is there primarily to preach to it. And yet

Christensen is very political indeed in his dislike of the welfare state (because it takes away the individual's freedom to use money and *compels* people to love their neighbours!), and in his view of property rights as sacrosanct, he attacks liberal protestants for their use of political action, and says that guidance for individual Christian social action comes through immediate communication by the Holy Spirit. Again, Sir Fred Catherwood, the leading evangelical industrialist, sees the 'dignity and freedom of the individual' to be the guiding light of Christian action, and sees the respect shown for individuals in British society as the result of Christian influence. Catherwood writes of the Christian ideal, but the ideal as it emerges seems to be a *description* of the British economic system and the trends at work within it. In fact, Catherwood insists that the aims we pursue *must* be compatible with the system. 'Above all their aims must be realizable in practice and should therefore be fulfilled by adapting the existing system rather than uprooting it.'[27]

Now the result of this narrowing of the gospel demands is clear. When the individual becomes the sole focus of the gospel, the new age only invades the old at the individual level. The biblical concern with social grace and social salvation disappears: terms like 'body', 'humanity', 'race', and 'nation' are not part of the evangelical working vocabulary. The stress is instead on 'the individual' and 'the Christian'. It is perhaps because of this that the tendency has been to see the heretical sects as the primary enemies of the gospel rather than political systems which may be seen as morally neutral. Indeed capitalism is positively valued for its toleration of religion.

(v) *A low view of the sacraments and the collapse of transcendence.* Again there are parallels in political life. One could argue that the liturgical renewal has brought the dimension of *social democracy* into the sacraments. So we come as equals, in fellowship, and share a common meal. But the *revolutionary* tradition seems to have gone, with its sense of sacramental life being a foretaste of the new world, the place where real transformation, real change, takes place. So the sacraments come to reinforce rather than to question or to undermine our social values. In fact, just as in our view of the Kingdom, so in sacramental theology, we need to see the combination of continuity and discontinuity. There is a continuity with this world. The Eucharist presupposes the goodness and Godward movement of creation. As Irenaeus said, writing of the created world, if the creation is merely decay, ignorance, and passion, then it is a sin against God to offer him the fruits of sin, ignorance, and passion. But there is also a discontinuity with a disordered and unjust order. So the Eucharist is concerned with the transformation of material structures and of human society. It is this element of change and conflict which has been reduced so that our modern liturgies are often reformist. We need to see worship, especially sacramental worship, as an end in itself: the offering of life and the evaluation of life as an end, and the rejection of the functional view of the human person by which he is valued for what he possesses, whether of money or skills. The revolutionary character of Christian worship lies in its rejection of the alienated and alienating view of man which lies at the heart of our present economic order.

So a theological renewal will involve a recovery of mysticism, of materialism, of humanism, of socialism, and of transcendence in worship. A tall order, and one which will be working against many of the trends of the present day. In the Catholic tradition of the Church of England there are strong negative indications. Much of what is seen as 'renewal' may be a nostalgia for a return to the ghetto. Richard Holloway several years ago warned of the danger for Anglicans that 'we simply stoke up our thuribles, stand in front of our golden reredoses, lock the doors against the cries and hectic laughter of those outside, and take a glory trip.'[28] His fears are not without some basis. Yet such a distortion would be fatal and could represent the death of the movement for 'Catholic Renewal' in the Church of England. It is worth remembering, and taking to heart, the words of Maurice Reckitt in the centenary year of the Oxford Movement in 1933:

> Men may celebrate no second centenary of our movement if we do not determine now to stand in social or in doctrinal issues plainly upon our own ground with a message and a philosophy for the whole range of human life and a true order of ends and means which men may reject indeed but the distinctive character of which they can no longer mistake.[29]

Notes

CHAPTER 1

Christian Social Action: Its Theological Basis

1 C. René Padilla (ed.), *The New Face of Evangelicalism* (Hodder and Stoughton 1976). For a complete report see J. D. Douglas (ed.), *Let the Earth Hear His Voice*. (Minneapolis 1975).

2 Padilla, op. cit., pp. 11, 12, 89. For the full text see Ronald J. Sider (ed.) *The Chicago Declaration* (Carol Stream, Creation House, 1974).

3 Cited in Padilla pp. 93–4. For the Radical Discipleship statement see Douglas op. cit., pp. 1294–6.

4 The cause of the disestablishment of the Church of England, according to Prebendary John Pearce, Chairman of the Church Society and a leading 'radical' evangelical, 'cannot be an evangelical one. To abandon a nation to the ravages of secularism neither advances the Gospel nor demonstrates Christian neighbour love' (letter in *The Times*, 10th April 1980).

5 See, for example, the widely used book by the thoughtful and respected Anglican evangelical J. N. D. Anderson, *Into the World* (Falcon Books 1968). Anderson stresses the doctrine of creation over against those of Incarnation, redemption and the church, as the foundation of Christian social responsibility (p. 15). While critical of older evangelical pietism, he still carries much of it with him, and his view of the Kingdom of God is very weak.

6 The question of the social thrust of the Charismatic renewal is a difficult one. Attempts to evolve a 'charismatic social theology' are very thin and disappointing. Apart from the appalling book by Larry Christensen *A Charismatic Approach to Social Action* (Lakeland 1975), see Paul Felton 'Towards a charismatic social theology' in *Theological Renewal* February–March 1978 pp. 22–29. A typical example of mainstream Anglican Charismatic social outlook is Michael Harper's 'Sickness in the church' in *Church Times*, 21st September 1979, where he attacks 'politicisation of the Gospel' and 'pseudo-prophecy'. In a subsequent article Harper agrees with E. R. Norman's description of Third World Christianity as 'spiritual and not political' (ibid 28th September 1979). Of course, the movement presents different aspects in different parts of the world. Writing from experience in Czechoslovakia, Dr Josif Smolik refers to a 'flight from responsibility' and 'a reactionary aspect, turning people away from the issues of responsibility in the world, into themselves, into an inner pietism, into an introverted, narrow world of the church without reference to secular society' (*Mainstream 4*, Spring 1977, p. 4). Some, however, would be hopeful that Charismatic renewal might contain the seeds of a new radicalism. Richard Russell has argued that 'the hope of the reforma-

tion of Evangelicalism appears to be in the Reformational Movement (stemming from Kuyperian Dutch Calvinism) and the Charismatic Movement conjointly, linking together a vision of the Kingdom of God with great expectations of the power of the Holy Spirit' (Richard Russell, 'The Growing Crisis of the Evangelical Worldview and its Resolution'. MA Thesis, University of Bristol, 1973.) For further discussion of the social dimensions of Charismatic renewal see Cardinal Suenens and Dom Helder Camara, *Charismatic Renewal and Social Action – a Dialogue* (Darton, Longman and Todd, 1980). See also the discussion in Chapter 9 of this volume.

7 See Dean M. Kelley, *Why Conservative Churches Are Growing* (Harper and Row 1977 edn). For an account of the popular 90-minute evangelical talk-show, Pat Robertson's '700 Club', see Russ Williams, 'Heavenly Message, Earthly Designs' in *Sojourners* September 1979.

8 Sider's writings are mainly published in the United States, but his important study *Rich Christians in an Age of Hunger* (Hodder and Stoughton 1978) has made him well known in Britain. His earlier article on *Evangelism, Salvation and Social Justice*, originally published in 1975, is now available in Britain from Grove Booklets, Bramcote, Nottingham. Sider sees evangelism and social justice as distinct but equally important. He founded Evangelicals for Social Action, and was editor of the Chicago Declaration of Evangelical Social Concern referred to above. See Ronald J. Sider (ed.) *The Chicago Declaration* (Carol Stream, Creation House, 1974).

9 See John Howard Yoder, *The Politics of Jesus* (William B. Eerdmans, Grand Rapids, Michigan, 1972.)

10 See Jim Wallis, *Agenda for Biblical People* (Harper and Row, 1976) and the monthly magazine *Sojourners* (1309 L St W, Washington DC 20005.)

11 Sider interviewed in *Third Way*, 13th January 1977.

12 Robert M. Price, 'A fundamentalist social gospel?' *Christian Century*, 28th November 1979.

13 Wallis, *Agenda for Biblical People* pp. 11–12.

14 *Post-American* 3:5 (June-July 1974) p. 24.

15 Jim Parker in *Post-American* 3:8 (November 1974) p. 14.

16 *Sojourners* 9:1 (January 1980) p. 11.

17 Jeremy Rifkin and Ted Howard, *The Emerging Order: God in an Age of Scarcity* (G. P. Putnam's Sons, 1979).

18 David Sheppard, *Built As A City* (Hodder and Stoughton 1974) For a radical evangelical critique of this book see John Bennington in *Crusade*, April 1974.

19 In his obituary for Downham, Peter Johnston, then Vicar of Islington and a leading Conservative Evangelical, noted that the early 1960s was, 'a period when Evangelicals had very little concern about the social implications of the Gospel . . . There had been a reaction against the so-called "Social Gospel" which seemed to ignore the message of personal salvation. Today's Evangelicals are far more conscious of the

social implications of the Gospel, and in this Denis was a pioneer.' (*Newsletter of Spitalfields Crypt* 18, Winter 1979).

20 David O. Moberg, *The Great Reversal* (Scripture Union 1972).

21 Richard F. Lovelace, *Dynamics of Spiritual Life* (Paternoster 1979) p. 400. Lovelace's book contains a useful section on the relationship of spirituality and social action. See especially Chapter 12 'The Spiritual Roots of Christian Social Concern' pp. 355–400. He stresses the fact that 'Evangelicals cannot recover their own wholeness and vitality, or prevent the loss of their own offspring to humanism or liberalism until they recover their social dynamic. Christians concerned for social action, both Evangelical and non-Evangelical, cannot reach their goals without general spiritual renewal' (p. 400). For a general, though now slightly dated, survey of the whole field of evangelical social thought see Derek J. Tidball, *Contemporary Evangelical Social Thinking: A Review* (Shaftesbury Project, 8 Oxford Street, Nottingham, 1977). A book which had considerable influence on the British scene, and which provided the title for the leading evangelical journal in the field, was Os Guinness's *The Dust of Death* (Inter Varsity Press 1973). There Guinness called for a 'Third Way', a 'constructive Christian radicalism' (pp. 369, 370.)

22 Chris Sugden in *Third Way*, 30th June 1977 p. 7.

23 Richard Zuercher in *Third Way*, March 1980 p. 31.

24 Conrad Noel, *Jesus the Heretic* (Religious Book Club 1939) p. 2.

25 Geevarghese Mar Ostathios, *Theology of a Classless Society* (Lutterworth Press 1979) pp. 11, 18, 24. The English theologian David Jenkins also stresses the importance of Trinitarian doctrine as the basis for social and political action. See his 'Doctrines which drive one to politics' in *Christian Faith and Political Hopes* (ed. Haddon Willmer, Epworth 1979) pp. 139–155. See also the valuable article by Thomas D. Parker, 'The political meaning of the doctrine of the Trinity: some theses', *Journal of Religion* (University of Chicago Divinity School 60:2 April 1980 pp. 165–184). Parker argues that 'the political meaning of the doctrine of the Trinity comes as an invitation to share in the struggle for that form of human community which expresses the truth symbolised in Christian faith in God the blessed Trinity' (p. 182).

26 See *De Carni Resurrectione* 8; *Adv. Marcion* 3:8.

27 *In Ephes. Hom.* 3:2

28 *Catech.* 18:23.

29 *The Body* (SCM Press 1961) p. 9

30 Arthur Vogel, *Is the Last Supper Finished?* (New York 1968) p. 64.

31 *Our Present Duty* (Golden Jubilee edition, Church Literature Association, 7 Tufton Street, London SW1, 1973).

32 But see Stanley Evans, *The Church in the Back Streets* (Mowbrays 1962) Chapter 2, 'The church as servant' for its use before Robinson.

33 *Letters and Papers from Prison* (1956 edn) p. 180; John A. T. Robinson, *Honest to God* (SCM Press 1963) p. 135.

34 See Alan Richardson, article 'preaching' in *A Theological Wordbook of the Bible* (1975 edn) p. 172.

35 For a valuable summary and critique of the 'servant church' idea see Michael Ramsey's contribution to *The Charismatic Christ* (ed. R. E. Terwilliger. Darton Longman and Todd 1974) p. 39f: 'It is in the context of the "Church for the world" theme that we frequently hear the church described as the servant. No longer does the church enjoy the position of cultural dominance it once enjoyed in western society. It needs to be more aware of this than it sometimes realizes, and to be less ready to use the world's privileges as its props. But the servant concept divides into a superficial notion, which is all too prominent, and a deeper notion, which is theologically based. It is not for the church to serve the world by offering the world solutions to its problems as the world itself sees them. Rather does the church serve the world by teaching it unpalatable truths and witnessing to its need for re-creation. But the true and positive meaning of the servant concept is that the church tries not just to draw people within its own religious activities, but to enter the situations in which people live and try to transform some of the world's behaviour into Christian behaviour.'

36 *An Anthology of the Love of God* (Mowbrays 1953) p. 123f.

37 Martin Luther King, *Strength to Love* (Fontana 1972 edn) p. 62: 'The church must be reminded that it is not the master or the servant of the state, but rather the conscience of the state. It must be the guide and critic of the state, and never its tool. If the church does not recapture its prophetic zeal, it will become an irrelevant social club without moral or spiritual authority.'

38 J. Lindblom, *Prophecy in Ancient Israel* (1962) p. 121.

39 See P. E. T. Widdrington in *The Return of Christendom* (Allen and Unwin 1922) p. 95: 'the revival of the Kingdom as the regulative principle of our theology'. Widdrington goes on: 'The call today is to return to what the New Testament calls "the Gospel of the Kingdom" – the Kingdom of God, the cardinal doctrine of our preaching, regulative of our theology, and the touchstone by which all the activities of the church are tested.' (p. 108).

CHAPTER 2
Catholic Theology and Social Change

1 For a detailed examination of the 'far right' Christian groups, both of Catholic and Protestant origin, see Derrick Knight, *Beyond the Pale* (Kogan Page 1980). Most of the books which attack the Vatican for its Leftist stance are obtainable through Augustine Publishing Company (formerly Britons Publishing Company), Chawleigh, Chumleigh, Devon. There is a variety of small Lefebvre-type groups, such as The Catholic Cross of Sanderstead, Surrey. Its leader, Major Leonard Hurst, speaks of the 'new post-Vatican 2 religion of Roman-Marxism'. For the claim that English Catholic leaders have been over influenced by the left see Ronald Butt, 'Immigration, and the dangers of the Catholic Church listening to the Left', *The Times*, 19 January 1978. For a hostile account of the changes since Vatican 2 see John Eppstein, *The*

Cult of Revolution in the Church (Valiant Publishers, Sandton, South Africa, undated). This volume, originally published in the USA in 1974, is widely used by right-wing groups as part of their ammunition. The claim that the Vatican has 'gone Marxist' is not new, nor restricted to the lunatic fringe of Catholic fundamentlism. Cf. Paul Johnson, 'Vatican and Kremlin', *New Statesman*, 12 November 1965. Referring to Vatican 2's call for sweeping social changes, Johnson says that it 'seems to presuppose a new doctrine of the perfectibility of human society which is not altogether unlike Marxism'. It is 'a call for positive social action which has a striking Marxist ring about it' (p. 726.).

2 Paras 30, 55. *Gaudium et Spes* is a crucial document for understanding the subsequent changes and their theological basis. For further study of the social theology of Vatican 2 and its implications see Gregory Baum, *The Social Imperative* (Paulist Press 1979) and Giancarlo Zizola, *The Utopia of Pope John XXIII* (Maryknoll, Orbis, 1980 edn). John's aim, says this writer, was 'to shift the center of the Catholic religious phenomenon from the ecclesiastical institution to man's historical consciousness' (p. 363).

3 Burns and Oates 1962 edn. p. xv.

4 Charles Marson in *Vox Clamantium* (ed. A. Reid) (A. D. Innes, 1894) p. 201. The whole of Marson's essay 'The Social Teachings of the Early Fathers' (pp. 198–224) should be read. For other examples of the use of the early Fathers by Anglo-Catholic socialists see Conrad Noel, *Socialism in Church History* (Frank Palmer 1910) pp. 91–114; and Jack Putterill, 'The hall-mark of sharing' in *The Return to Reality* (ed. S. G. Evans) (Zeno Press 1954) pp. 34–63.

5 *The Faces of God* (Geoffrey Chapman 1975) p. 164.

6 For the thinking of the Christendom Group see Maurice Reckitt, *Faith and Society* (Longmans 1932) and *Prospect for Christendom* (ed. Maurice Reckitt, Faber, 1945).

7 *City of God* 1.

8 For similar slogans in the 'Call to the Nation' of Archbishop Coggan, see Herbert McCabe in *New Blackfriars*, November 1975, pp. 482–3, 492. Noting that the Archbishop didn't tell people to 'pull together' or not to 'rock the boat', McCabe comments: 'but these seem to be almost his only omissions from the catalogue of clerical banalities.' (p. 482).

9 *Osservatore Romano*, 10 June 1944. On the Catholic Church and Nazism see Guenter Lewy, *The Catholic Church and Nazi Germany* (Weidenfeld and Nicolson 1964).

10 Hastings op. cit p. 36.

11 On the history of the Catholic Worker movement see William D. Miller, *A Harsh and Dreadful Love: Dorothy Day and the Catholic Worker* (Darton, Longman and Todd 1973) and Robert Coles, *A Spectacle unto the World: The Catholic Worker Movement* (Viking Press, New York 1973). The atmosphere of the movement is best captured by reading the monthly *Catholic Worker* (36 East First Street, New York, NY 10003) and from Peter Maurin, *Easy Essays* (Chicago, Franciscan Herald Press 1977 edn).

12 Paras 31, 33.

13 Hastings op. cit. p. 35.

14 For the general social thought of Pope John Paul II see Roger Hazelton, 'Redeeming humanity: the Pope's theological vision', *Christian Century*, 3 October 1979, pp. 945–8.

15 See Stephen Fay, 'The priest who thinks the Pope is a Protestant' *Sunday Times*, 19 September 1976. According to P. A. Allum, 'The conservative at the Vatican gates', *New Society*, 17 August 1978, pp. 349–50, Lefebvre is 'a self-confessed fascist'. For the general background of the French right see Douglas Johnson, 'The new Right in France', *New Society*, 12 June 1980, pp. 206–8; and J. S. McClelland, (ed.) *The French Right* (Cape 1970).

16 Paras 31–32. On the "justum bellum" tradition see Roland Bainton, *Christian Attitudes to War and Peace* (Nashville, Abingdon Press, 1960); Paul Ramsey, *War and the Christian Conscience* (Duke University Press 1961) and *The Just War* (New York, Scribners, 1968); and Robert McAfee Brown, *Religion and Violence* (Westminster Press, Philadelphia 1973).

17 There is now a massive literature on liberation theology in English. From a large selection, see José Miguez-Bonino, *Revolutionary Theology Comes of Age* (SPCK 1975); José P. Miranda, *Marx and the Bible: A Critique of the Philosophy of Oppression* (SCM Press 1977); J. L. Segundo, *The Liberation of Theology* (Maryknoll, Orbis, 1976); and Leonardo Boff, *Jesus Christ Liberator* (Orbis 1978). For good accounts by or for western readers see Alfredo Fierro, *The Militant Gospel* (SCM Press 1977); Robert McAfee Brown, *Theology in a New Key* (Westminster Press, Philadelphia 1978); and J. Andrew Kirk, *Liberation Theology: An Evangelical View from the Third World* (Marshall, Morgan and Scott 1979) and *Theology Encounters Revolution* (Inter Varsity Press 1980). For collections of key texts see Alistair Kee (ed.) *A Reader in Political Theology* (SCM Press 1974) and *The Scope of Political Theology* (SCM Press 1978); and Rosino Gibellini (ed.) *Frontiers of Theology in Latin America* (SCM Press 1980). But the most valuable study of the relationship of liberation theology with the thought of Vatican 2 remains Gustavo Gutierrez, *A Theology of Liberation* (Orbis 1973).

18 On the context and meaning of St Bernard's poem see Conrad Noel's chapter 'Strangers and Pilgrims' in *Jesus the Heretic* (Religious Book Club, 1939) pp. 59–65. Noel comments:
'. . . what is remarkable about it for our own generation is that the hymns we used to consider as relating to the world beyond death, are integral parts of this poem, largely concerned with the hope of the new world order, which we thought had been lost for so many centuries and left for us to rediscover.' (p.62).

19 John R. Griffin, 'The radical phase of the Oxford Movement' *Journal of Ecclesiastical History* 27:1 (1976) pp. 47–48. See also his 'John Keble Radical', *Anglican Theological Review* 53 (1971) pp. 167ff.

20 *Our Present Duty* (Church Literature Association, 1973 edn)

21 N. P. Williams and Charles Harris (ed) *Northern Catholicsm* (1933).

22 This combination was an important element in the schism which led to the creation of the Anglican Catholic Church (formerly the Anglican Church of North America). One of the leaders of the group wrote in 1977, prior to his secession from the Episcopal Church, that 'our spirituality is utterly different from Rome's'. He went on: 'Anglo-Catholics however have not followed these recent changes. Owing to this fact we are virtually the only branch of Western Christianity in the United States that explicitly stands for beauty and transcendence in liturgy . . . There is an unmistakable Anglo-Catholic consciousness and it cannot be reduced to anything else' (C. D. Keyes in *American Church News*, January 1977, p. 5).

23 For Thaxted's devotion to the Flag of St George and rejection of the Union Jack see Conrad Noel, *The Battle of the Flags* (Labour Publishing Company 1922), and, for the wider background, Reg Groves, *Conrad Noel and the Thaxted Movement* (Merlin Press, 1967).

24 Richard Hooker, *Of the Laws of Ecclesiastical Polity* VIII. 1, 2, 5. in *Works . . . of Richard Hooker* ed. J. Keble, Oxford 1841. III. pp. 330ff.

25 C. B. Moss, *Anglo-Catholicism at the Cross Roads* (Faith Press 1933) p. 3.

26 *Loughborough Conference Report* (Church Literature Association, 1979) pp. 33, 36.

CHAPTER 3
Believing in the Incarnation and Its Consequences

1 T. Paul Verghese, *The Freedom of Man* (Philadelphia, Westminster Press 1972) p. 55.

2 ibid. Cf. M. D. Chenu in *Western Spirituality: Historical Roots, Ecumenical Routes* (ed. Matthew Fox, Notre Dame, Fides/Claretian, 1979) p. 200: 'When it comes to discussing passion and spirituality, Christians should not forget the fact that Augustine was a victim of Manicheism for no small part of his life and that all life long he was haunted by an unusually negative experience of uncontrolled passion. Aquinas' spirituality does not operate out of so sad a personal experience. Aquinas is not guilt-ridden at being a human being and not an angel.'

3 Verghese op. cit. pp. 55–6.

4 *In Joan. Evang*. 23. For Augustine the essence of the fall is the disordering of rational control over the body and its feelings. He looks particularly at the male erection and sexual libido as the seat of the fallen and disordered state of humanity. So in this fallen state, it is impossible to engage in sexual intercourse, even within marriage, without sin, for there is a necessary accompaniment of lust. Thus every child becomes tainted with original sin. Rosemary Ruether points out that in Augustine the image of God is not only associated with the mind but also with the male principle. 'In Augustine the image of God becomes more specifically a male principle. The domination of male over female is seen as analogous to the domination of mind over body. This leads Augustine even to deny that women possess the image of God autonomously, in their own right. 'The woman possesses the

image of God only when taken together with the male who is her head. In herself alone, however, she symbolises the bodily principle that must be subordinate to its head, the male.' (in *Western Spirituality*, op. cit. p. 148.) See *De Trinitate* 7.7.10.

5 Sebastian Moore. *God Is A New Language* (Darton, Longman and Todd, 1967) p. 80.

6 C. S. Lewis, *Christian Behaviour* (1943) p. 45. For a similarly pessimistic view of man and of human potential see E. R. Norman, *Christianity and the World Order* (Oxford, 1979). Norman refers to the 'doctrine of man' (p. 11) and claims that religion 'conveys a unique understanding of human life' (ibid). Specifically, he suggests that there is 'a particularly Christian understanding of the nature of man and his social state' (p. 56), and that 'religion is centred . . . on the facts of human nature' (p. 76). This involves, apparently, 'a sense of the ultimate worthlessness of human expectations of a better life on earth' (pp. 19–20) and of 'human fallibility . . . the worthlessness of all earthly expectations' (p. 14).

7 paras 12, 41.

8 1 John 4:2. Recently the centrality, and indeed the truth, of the Incarnation has come under fire from so-called 'radical' theologians. Cf. John Hick (ed.) *The Myth of God Incarnate*. (SCM Press 1977). Although Professor Maurice Wiles argues in this volume that a 'Christianity without incarnation' would not be a non-incarnational faith in the broad sense (p. 7), it is clear from his other writings that he rejects the *specific* and *particular* character of the Incarnation of Christ. See his *The Re-making of Christian Doctrine* (SCM Press 1974.) On this book and its implications for Christian orthodoxy see Colin Gunton's discussion in *Theology* 77:654 (December 1974) pp. 619–624.

9 J. A. T. Robinson, *The Body* (SCM Press 1961 edn) pp. 9, 51.

10 2 Peter 1:4.

11 1 John 3:9.

12 Irenaeus, *Adv. Haer.* 5.

13 *De Incarnatione* 54:3. It seems to me correct to refer to this tradition as one of 'deification', provided that we are clear what is not being stated. E. L. Mascall has stressed that 'there is a persistent tradition in Christian thought which finds it impossible to do justice to the transformation that a human being undergoes when he is incorporated into Christ except by saying that he is *deified*' (*Via Media*, Longmans 1957, p. 121). Mascall uses the term 'Deified Creaturehood' (see ibid, Chapter Four, pp. 121–165.) Rowan Williams has stressed that 'it is of first importance to bear in mind that "deification" for Origen, Athanasius and their successors did not mean a sharing in the divine "substance", a quasi-physical participation, but enjoying the divine *relation* of Son to Father, sharing the divine life'. (*The Wound of Knowledge*, Darton, Longman and Todd 1979, p. 49). For a critical evaluation of the 'deification' tradition, see Ben Drewery, 'Deification' in *Christian Spirituality: Essays in Honour of Gordon Rupp* (SCM Press 1975) pp. 33–62.

14 *Or. 2 adv. Ar.* 21:70.

15 *De Carni Resurrectione* 8; *Adv. Marcion* 3:8.

16 Paul Evdokimov, *L'Orthodoxie*, p. 113. On the eastern tradition see Vladimir Lossky, *The Mystical Theology of the Eastern Church* (James Clarke 1957).

17 Sebastian Moore op. cit p. 59.

18 Georges Khodre, cited in *Jesus Christ Frees and Unites* (5th Assembly of the World Council of Churches, 1975, Section 5, p. 35).

19 1 John 4:2.

20 Herbert Marcuse, 'Marxism and the new humanity: an unfinished revolution' in John C. Raines and Thomas Dean (eds) *Marxism and Radical Religion: Essays Towards a Revolutionary Humanism* (Philadelphia, Temple University Press, 1970) p. 7.

21 Inscription on Gandhi's place of cremation at Rajghat.

22 *Pedagogy of the Oppressed* (Penguin 1972) pp. 43–4.

23 *The Joyous Cosmology* (New York, Random House, 1962) pp. 70, 72.

24 *Human Energy* (1969 edn) p. 50.

25 *The Future of Man* (1964) pp. 143–4.

26 *The Return of the Father* (1875) p. 49. Cf. Juan Luis Segundo, in a passage strikingly similar to Hancock's, says that in these early centuries, 'something of radical importance for the history of humanity was decided under the apparent form of a "theological" controversy' (cited in Alfred T. Hennelly, *Theologies in Conflict*, Maryknoll, Orbis, 1979, p. 147.)

27 *Immigration and Enoch Powell* (Tom Stacey, 1970) pp. 69, 70. For the claim that Powell is perhaps a Monophysite see Martin Jarrett-Kerr's review of *No Easy Answers* in *The Guardian*, 27 September 1973. J. K. Mozley stressed the ethical consequences of the Monophysite heresy: for if Christ had no truly human will, then his example is valueless and obedience impossible. Cf. *The Doctrine of the Incarnation* (Bles 1949) p. 85.

28 J. A. T. Robinson, *The Human Face of God* (SCM Press 1973) p. 7.

29 *Modern Man in Search of a Soul* (1933) p. 238.

30 *Contra Celsum* 1:32. Rowan Williams, *The Wound of Knowledge* (1979) p. 25 speaks of the 'reduction of salvation to spiritual technology'. 'To make salvation a matter of "saving truths" is to yield the pass to the gnostic, sidestepping entirely the process of healing and integrating the whole of the human person.' (p. 29.)

31 R. M. Grant, *Gnosticism and Early Christianity* (1966) pp. 8–9.

32 Rollo May, *Power and Innocence* (Souvenir Press 1972) passim.

33 ibid p. 50.

34 Rowan Williams rightly says that 'the Arian God cannot be directly involved at all in the work of salvation' (op. cit. p. 48), and that 'Athanasius' case depends upon the capacity of God to involve himself in the historical order' (p. 49).

35 *Hist. Ar.* 62. Against this view, Don Cupitt has recently argued that it was orthodox Christology which helped pave the way for authoritarian-

ism. 'Early Christianity had repudiated the Emperor cult, but now conciliar Christianity came increasingly to be modelled on the Emperor cult.' (in his essay 'The Christ of Christendom' in *The Myth of God Incarnate* ed. John Hick, SCM Press 1977, p. 139.) This led, in Cupitt's view, to 'a world-view which stressed continuity, hierarchy and due obedience . . . Christ crowned the Emperor, one a step higher in the scale of being merely stooping slightly to bestow authority upon one a step lower' (ibid. p. 140). This view, of course, depends heavily on Eusebius with his notorious 'one God . . . one sovereign' teaching, in which monotheism and monarchy were allied (*The Oration of Eusebius Pamphili in Praise of the Emperor Constantine*, III.5f.) But Eusebius's Christology, as Colin Gunton has pointed out, shows 'a marked christological subordinationism' ('The political Christ: some reflections on Mr. Cupitt's thesis', *Scottish Journal of Theology* 32 (1979) p. 525. See the whole article, pp. 521–540 for a strong and impressive critique of Cupitt.) While Gunton accepts that the development of the 'Christ of Christendom' does owe much to the teaching that Jesus is the heavenly Lord, he makes an important distinction between the Christ of Christendom, or the Constantinian Christ, and the Christ of Chalcedon. So far from encouraging the development of the former, there were features in Chalcedonian orthodoxy which strongly militate against it. 'The imperial Christ was a product of dogmatic divinity abstracted from the gospel accounts of the human Jesus. When the divinity was separated from the humanity it became possible to adapt the doctrine of the divinity of Christ to the political needs of the day, but only by ignoring the demand made by the very Chalcedonian christology that was being hammered out at the same time. In terms of the doctrine of God, this made for a naked monotheism, with all its possibilities for absolutism . . . Kierkegaard saw the point of Chalcedon better than Don Cupitt. Far from teaching a general synthesis of the divine and the human – the bringing of God down to earth or the elevation of man to divinity in the triumphalism of Christendom – its teaching implies that there has happened here what cannot happen otherwise. That is both the offence of orthodox christology, of which Don Cupitt wishes to relieve us, and its teaching that no political power can be identified with the Kingdom of God' (Gunton, p. 537.) Cf. also Thomas D. Parker 'The political meaning of the doctrine of the Trinity: some theses', *Journal of Religion* 60:2 (April 1980) pp. 165–184.

36 Hancock, op. cit. pp. 48f.

37 S. D. Headlam, *The Service of Humanity and Other Sermons* (1882)

38 *Against the Self-Images of the Age* (Duckworth 1971) p. 26.

39 *Treatise on Prayer* 60.

40 Revelations of Divine Love 55, 56.

41 Sebastian Moore, op. cit. p. 80.

42 *Adv. Haer.* 4.

43 *On Icons* 1:16.

44 Sam Keen, *To a Dancing God* (Fontana 1970) Chapter Five, p. 142.

45 ibid p. 153.

46 ibid p. 155.
47 Moore, op. cit. p. 36.
48 Lossky, op. cit. pp. 65, 67.

CHAPTER 4
Contemplation and Resistance as seen in the Spirituality of Thomas Merton

1 *America is Hard to Find* (SPCK 1973) pp. 77, 78.
2 ibid p. 56.
3 'Contemplation and Resistance', *Peace News* 18 May 1973.
4 Gustavo Gutierrez, *A Theology of Liberation* (SCM Press 1974) p. 204. See also Alfred T. Hennelly, *Theologies in Conflict* (Maryknoll, Orbis 1979) pp. 140–156; and Segundo Galilea, 'Liberation as an encounter with politics and contemplation', *Concilium 96: The Mystical and Political Dimension of the Christian Faith* (New York, Herder and Herder, 1974).
5 *Where the Wasteland Ends* (Faber 1972) p. xxiii.
6 Alistair Kee, (ed) *Seeds of Liberation* (SCM Press 1973) p. vii.
7 cited in Gerald Twomey (ed) *Thomas Merton: Prophet in the Belly of a Paradox* (New York, Paulist Press 1978) p. 1.
8 Preface to *Contemplation in a World of Action* (New York, Doubleday, Image Books 1973) p. 12.
9 cited in George Woodcock, *Thomas Merton, Monk and Poet* (Edinburgh, Canongate 1978) p. 5.
10 E. Glenn Hinson, 'The Catholicising of Contemplation: Thomas Merton's Place in the Church's Prayer Life', *Perspectives in Religion* 1:2 (Summer 1973) cited in Raymond Bailey, *Thomas Merton on Mysticism* (New York, Doubleday, Image Books, 1975) p. 17.
11 *The Prison Meditations of Father Alfred Delp* (1963) p. 95.
12 *Faith and Violence* (University of Notre Dame Press 1968) p. 52.
13 ibid.
14 James W. Douglass, *Resistance and Contemplation* (New York, Doubleday 1972) p. 139.
15 *Contemplative Prayer* (Darton, Longman and Todd 1973) p. 135.
16 *Conjectures of a Guilty Bystander* (Sheldon Press, 1977) p. 58.
17 *Contemplative Prayer* p. 111.
18 *Thoughts in Solitude* (Burns and Oates 1958) p. 86.
19 *Conjectures . . .* p. 10.
20 *Raids on the Unspeakable* (New York, New Directions 1966) p. 18.
21 *The Sign of Jonas* (Sheldon Press 1976 edn) p. 268.
22 *Contemplative Prayer* pp. 25–26.
23 *Raids on the Unspeakable* p. 172.
24 Tolbert McCarroll, 'A quiet life: the contemporary spiritual significance of Father Louis Merton', *Cistercian Studies* 8:3 (1973) p. 198.
25 Daniel Berrigan, *No Bars to Manhood* (New York, Mentor 1970) p. 139.

26 On Merton's social doctrine see James T. Baker, *Thomas Merton: Social Critic* (Lexington, University of Kentucky Press 1971); D. Q. McInerny, *Thomas Merton and Society* (Ann Arbor, Michigan, University Microfilm 1969); and F. J. Kelly, *Man Before God: Thomas Merton on Social Responsibility* (New York, Doubleday 1974).

27 *Spiritual Direction and Meditation* (Anthony Clarke 1975 edn) p. 62.

28 cited in John J. Higgins, *Thomas Merton on Prayer* (New York, Image Books 1975) p. 19.

29 *Mystics and Zen Masters* (New York, Farrar, Straus and Giroux 1969) p. 153.

30 *Zen and the Birds of Appetite* (New York, New Directions 1968) p. 75.

31 *Disputed Questions* (Hollis and Carter 1961) p. x.

32 PG 44:1137B.

33 T. Paul Verghese, *The Freedom of Man* (Philadelphia, Westminster Press 1972) p. 54.

34 Henri J. M. Nouwen, *Pray to Live* (Notre Dame, Fides 1972) p. 54.

35 *The Asian Journal of Thomas Merton* (Sheldon Press 1974) p. 329.

36 cited in Twomey op. cit. p. 84.

37 *Contemplative Prayer* p. 25.

38 *Asian Journal* p. 341.

39 *Seeds of Destruction* (New York, Farrar, Straus and Giroux 1964) pp. 170–1.

40 *Asian Journal* p. 317.

41 cited in *Thomas Merton Monk: a monastic tribute* (ed. Patrick Hart, Hodder and Stoughton 1974) p. 53.

42 ibid.

43 *Seasons of Celebration* (New York, Farrar, Straus and Giroux 1964) pp. 211–2.

44 cited in Woodcock op. cit. p. 117f.

45 ibid.

46 ibid p. 120.

47 *Conjectures* pp. 69–70.

48 ibid p. 72.

49 *Gandhi on Non-Violence* (New York, New Directions 1965) p. 13.

50 cited in Gerald Twomey (ed) *Thomas Merton: Prophet in the Belly of a Paradox* (New York, Paulist Press, 1978) p. 82.

51 *Raids on the Unspeakable* p. 22.

52 cited in Woodcock op. cit. p. 153.

53 Douglass op. cit. p. 66.

54 For Merton's understanding of Zen see his *Mystics and Zen Masters* (New York, Farrar, Straus and Giroux, 1969).

55 cited in William Johnston, *Christian Zen* (Harper and Row 1974 edn) p. 22.

56 *Conjectures* p. 148.

57 Douglass op. cit. pp. 9–10. Cf. Berrigan in Kee, op. cit. p. 88: 'The young people across the country are beginning to discover Merton all over again because maybe they have gone through the kind of enormous tunnel of the 60s and see the deadly quality of trying to create alternatives that have no inside to them . . . They are finding in him a tremendous range of understanding and depth that he could have spoken about the Cold War and the Hot War and the nuclear build-up and the racial crisis before they happened because he had a kind of extra-sensory apparatus functioning through his prayer, through his reading and pondering. Maybe he is going to help us to get a better balance of things.'

CHAPTER 5
Contemplation as a Subversive Activity

1 Cf. Jim Wallis, *Agenda for Biblical People* (Harper and Row 1976) p. lf: 'What matters most today is whether one is a supporter of establishment Christianity or a practitioner of biblical faith. Establishment Christianity has made its peace with the established order. It no longer feels itself to be in conflict with the pretensions of the state, with the designs of economic and political power, or with the values and style of life enshrined in the national culture. Establishment Christianity is a religion of accommodation and conformity, which values realism and success more than faithfulness and obedience. It is heavily invested in the political order, the social consensus, and the ideology of the economic system. Its leaders are more comfortable as chaplains than as prophets; its proclamation has been rendered harmless and inoffensive to the wealthy and powerful; and its churchly life has become a mere ecclesiastical reproduction of the values and assumptions of the surrounding environment . . . Given the strong biblical teaching concerning the fallen condition of the world, it is remarkable how easily the church has become cozy and comfortable with the powers of the world.'

2 On Péguy see Alan Ecclestone, 'Mystique and Politique', *Theology* 79:667 (January 1976) pp. 29–35.

3 Cf. Edward Norman, *Christianity and the World Order* (Oxford 1979) p.80: 'To contend, as I am doing, for the separation of individual Christian action from the corporate witness of the Church, and to regard Christianity as being by nature concerned primarily with the relationship of the soul to eternity, is these days denounced within Christian opinion as a "privatization" of religion. I think that is exactly what it is.'

4 R. D. Laing, *The Politics of Experience and The Bird of Paradise* (Penguin 1971 edn) p.118: 'There is a prophecy in Amos that there will be a famine in the land, not a famine for bread, nor a thirst for water, but of *hearing* the words of the Lord. That time has now come to pass. It is the present age.'

5 Theodore Roszak, *Where the Wasteland Ends* (Faber 1972) pp.134, 135.

6 According to recent official data, over ten million people were living in poverty in Britain in 1978 despite the doubling of real disposable

incomes since 1951. 'The poor', on the official estimate, comprised 23 per cent of all families in Britain, and one-fifth of the total population. While the percentage of wealth owned by the bottom half rose to 5 per cent, the wealthiest 10 per cent of the population still owned 61.1 per cent of wealth in 1977. (*Social Trends*, HMSO December 1979.) Moreover recent research has confirmed both the persistence of class inequalities and the structural (i.e. non-accidental) character of poverty in Britain. The relative chances of people of different social classes reaching the top have remained basically unchanged for sixty years (John H. Goldthorpe, *Social Mobility and Class Structure in Modern Britain*, Oxford 1980.) On the persistence of poverty as inequality see Peter Townsend, *Poverty in the United Kingdom: a survey of household resources and standards of living* (Penguin 1979).

The poverty issue is a test case for the social importance of contemplative awareness and perception. Cf. Charles Elliott, *Inflation and the Compromised Church* (Belfast, Christian Journals 1975), p.146: '. . . Christians can and surely must face in their own concrete situation the inequities and miseries with which they are surrounded. It is then that they begin to reflect the life of Christ and to foreshadow the life of his Kingdom. But they will reflect it only to the extent that they have seen it. Radical action begins with radical contemplation.' While the *reality* of poverty and inequality has increased, there is no evidence that the *consciousness* of this reality has increased to the same extent.

7 cited in David Lake, 'Simone Weil: Spirituality of the void' in *Ways of the Spirit* (SCM *Movement* Pamphlet 28, undated) p. 8.

8 Daniel Berrigan, *America Is Hard To Find* (SPCK 1973) pp.77–78.

9 Thomas Merton, *Contemplative Prayer* (Darton, Longman and Todd, 1973) p.25. See also the references to Chapter Four.

10 Thomas Merton, *Conjectures of a Guilty Bystander* (Sheldon Press, 1977) p.58.

11 St John of the Cross, *The Ascent of Mount Carmel* and *The Dark Night of the Soul*, available in various editions.

12 Roszak, op. cit. p. xxii.

13 Simone Weil, *Gateway to God* (Fontana, 1974) p.56.

14 *The Cloud of Unknowing* 49.

15 St John of the Cross, *The Living Flame of Love* 3:29–51.

16 *The Book of Supreme Truth* Chapter 4.

17 *The Adornment of the Spiritual Marriage* Chapter 66.

18 The full context of Marx's oft-quoted statement needs to be read in his *Critique of Hegel's Philosophy of Right*. See T. B. Bottomore (ed) *Karl Marx: Early Writings* (1963) pp.43–44.

19 Edwin Muir, 'One Foot in Eden' in *Collected Poems 1921–1958*.

CHAPTER 6
Spiritual Direction in the Present Climate

1 I. M. Lewis, *Ecstatic Religion* (Penguin 1971) p. 20.

2 For an account of the Soho period and the beginnings of the spiritual quest see my *Keep The Faith Baby* (SPCK 1972).

3 Max Thurian, *Confession* (1958) p. 69.

4 See my *Youthquake* (SPCK 1973) for a detailed account.

5 See R. D. Laing, *The Politics of Experience and The Bird of Paradise* (1971 edn), and other works.

6 Frank Lake, *Clinical Theology* (Darton Longman and Todd 1966); Westminster Pastoral Foundation, 23 Kensington Square, London W.8; Association of Pastoral Care and Counselling, c/o BAC, 26 Bedford Square, London WC1B 3HU.

7 See Frank Lake, *Clinical Pastoral Care in Schizoid Personality Reactions* (Clinical Theology Association, December 1970); Rollo May, *Love and Will* (1972 edn) and *Power and Innocence* (1974 edn).

8 See Roy Bailey and Mike Brake, *Radical Social Work* (1975).

9 Cf. the description of Tikhon in Dostoyevsky's *The Devils* (trans. David Magarshack, 1957 edn), p. 262.

10 See my *Soul Friend* (Sheldon Press, 1977).

11 E. W. Trueman Dicken, 'St John of the Cross and modern English spirituality' in *Mount Carmel* 19:1 (1971), p. 6.

12 Carl Wennerstrom in J. Luther Adams and Seward Hiltner (ed), *Pastoral Care in the Liberal Churches* (1970) pp. 37–38.

13 *English Spirituality* (1963) p. 11.

14 'Objections to a proposed national pastoral organisation' in *Contact* 35 (June 1971) pp. 25–26, 27.

15 Daniel Day Williams. *The Minister and the Cure of Souls* (1961) pp. 25–26.

16 *The Church in Sunderland*, Report of the Bishop's Commission 1971, p. 20.

CHAPTER 7
Spirituality, Psychotherapy, and Politics

1 Theodore Roszak, *Unfinished Animal* (Faber 1975) pp. 241–2.

2 ibid p. 242.

3 *Contact* 61 (1978)

4 *Zen in the Art of Helping* (Routledge 1976) pp. 32–3.

5 These aspects of friendship and freedom are emphasised in two recent studies on spiritual direction: Tilden Edwards, *Spiritual Friend* (New York, Paulist Press 1980), and John J. English, *Spiritual Freedom* (Guelph, Ontario, Loyola House 1975). Edwards has a helpful section on a course in direction which he has established in Washington. English is particularly concerned with the use of the Ignatian Exercises and their role in leading the Christian to freedom.

6 *Contact* Spring 1974 p. 38.

7 1979, p. 1.

8 Faber 1972, p. xxii.

CHAPTER 8
'Not Survival but Prophecy': The Future of Monasticism

1 R. E. Terwilliger in *The Charismatic Christ* (Darton, Longman and Todd 1974) p. 57

2 Andrew Greeley, *The Persistence of Religion* (SCM Press 1973) pp. 1, 3.

3 *Where the Wasteland Ends* (Faber 1972) p. 110.

4 *Thomas Merton on Peace* (New York, McCall Publishing Company 1971) pp. 160–2.

5 *The Faces of God* (Geoffrey Chapman 1975) p. 54.

6 See the references in Chapter 4.

7 *The Asian Journal of Thomas Merton* (Sheldon Press 1974) p. 329.

8 *Contemplative Prayer* (Darton, Longman and Todd 1973 edn) p. 25.

9 cited in *Thomas Merton, Monk: A Monastic Tribute* (ed. Patrick Hart, Hodder 1975) p. 53.

10 Ruth Glass, *Newcomers: The West Indians in London* (Centre for Urban Studies and George Allen and Unwin, 1960) pp. 133–4. For much earlier uses of the concept of marginality in urban sociology see Robert Park, 'Human migration and the marginal man', *American Journal of Sociology* 33 (1928), pp. 881–893, and other writings of the 'Chicago school' of urban sociologists.

11 Ruth Glass and John Westergaard, *London's Housing Needs* (Centre for Urban Studies 1965) p. 10.

12 *The Faces of God*, p. 21. It is interesting to note that Karl Barth, who was hardly a fanatical devotee of the monastic life, stressed that early desert monasticism was 'a highly responsible and effective protest and opposition to the world, and not least to a worldly church, a new and specific way of combating it, and therefore a direct address to it.' (*Church Dogmatics*, IV.2. p. 13.) For further discussion of the theme of monastic protest see Anthony Mullaney, 'The monastic tradition: the contemplative in a time of systems' in *Manna in the Wilderness* (SCM *Movement* Pamphlet 36, undated) pp. 9–13.

CHAPTER 9
The Charismatic Movement and the Demons

1 The subject is notoriously one which is characterised by gross exaggeration and absurd claims. For an extreme example cf. the statement by Billy Graham in *The Jesus Generation* (1971) p. 161: 'in England, a nation which many had thought of as perhaps the world's most rational society, a legislator now claims that a majority of the secondary school students have been in touch with either a witch or a wizard.' John Richards, in his useful book *But Deliver Us from Evil* (Darton, Longman and Todd 1974) p. 81 cites Billy Graham as if he were a reliable authority. For the background to the occult revival see my *Youthquake* (Sheldon Press 1973) Chapter Five.

2 The two cases of deaths which attracted most publicity were those heard at Leeds Crown Court in April 1975 and at the Old Bailey in September 1980.

3 John Pairman Brown, *The Liberated Zone* (SCM Press 1970) p. 99.

4 See 1 Cor. 2:6–8; Ephes. 6:12; Gal. 4:3; Col. 2:8.

5 See G. H. C. McGregor, 'Principalities and powers: the cosmic background to Paul's thought', *New Testament Studies* 1 (1954–5) pp. 17–28.

6 O. Cullman, *Christ and Time* (1950) p. 192.

7 See E. L. Mascall, *The Christian Universe* (Darton, Longman and Todd, 1966) Chapter Six, 'Unseen Warfare' pp. 109–130.

8 C. H. Dodd, *The Coming of Christ* p. 60. See also Herman Ridderbos, *The Coming of the Kingdom* (Philadelphia, Presbyterian and Reformed Publishing Company 1975) pp. 61–115.

9 O. Cullman, *The State in the New Testament* (1956) p. 102.

10 *The Secular City* (SCM Press 1965) p. 149. While the book is now very dated, Chapter Seven, 'The church as cultural exorcist', pp. 149–163, is still worth reading.

11 Geza Vermes, *Jesus the Jew* (Collins, 1973) p. 22.

12 Norman Perrin, *Rediscovering the Teaching of Jesus* (SCM Press 1967) p. 65.

13 See Romans 8:38f; 1 Corinthians 2:8; 15:24–26; Ephesians 1:20f; 2:1f; 3:10, 12; Colossians 1:16; 2:15, etc.

14 Hendrik Berkhof, *Christ and the Powers* (Scottdale, Pennsylvania, Herald Press 1977 edn) p. 23.

15 ibid. p. 66.

16 ibid. Further on the powers see Heinrich Schlier, *Principalities and Powers in the New Testament* (Herder 1962)

17 in 'The Angels of Darkness', BBC Radio 3 27th October 1975.

18 Dom Robert Petitpierre, OSB, *Exorcising Devils* (Robert Hale 1976) pp. 26, 37.

19 cited in T. S. Szasz, *The Manufacture of Madness* (Paladin 1973 edn), p. 102.

20 Rollo May, *Love and Will* (Fontana, 1972 edn) p. 123.

21 On this see Victor White, *God and the Unconscious* (Fontana 1967 edn) especially Chapter Ten, 'Devils and Complexes'.

22 in 'The Angels of Darkness' op. cit.

23 On exorcism in baptism see Jean Daniélou, *The Bible and the Liturgy* (1950); *Made Not Born* (Murphy Center for Liturgical Research, University of Notre Dame Press 1976); Alexander Schmemann, *Of Water and the Spirit* (St Vladimir's Seminary Press 1974), etc.

24 Schmemann, op. cit. pp. 24, 26.

25 Cf. the late Canon Stanley Evans on the revised baptism rite and catechism of the Church of England, On baptism: 'The word "world" has changed its meaning, and neither it nor its pomps are any more to be renounced by good Anglicans. At the Reformation the Church of England made enormous concessions to "the world": it has taken 400 years to have them finally enshrined in liturgical form.' (*Junction* 11, July 1960). On the catechism: 'The only public criticism of the revision

so far has been its elimination of the devil. Is it too much to say that its compromise with "the world", its failure to see all mankind redeemed in Christ, its elimination of helping the poor from the work of a deacon, and the whole tendency manifested by these things represents a retreat from fundamental Christian positions? And this is the very devil.' (*Junction* 14, April 1961.)

26 Reuben A. Sheares II, cited in Dibinga Wa Said, 'An African theology of decolonisation', *Harvard Theological Review* 64 (1971) p. 524.

27 James H. Cone, *God of the Oppressed* (SPCK 1975) p. 77.

28 Cardinal Suenens, 'The prince of darkness', *The Tablet*, 4th October 1980. Cf. also his letter in *The Times*, 18th September 1980.

29 letter in *The Times* op. cit.

30 J. Dominian, 'A psychological evaluation of the Pentecostal movement', *Expository Times* 87:10 (July 1976) p. 296.

31 ibid.

32 *Theological and Pastoral Orientations on the Catholic Charismatic Renewal* (Malines, Belgium, 21st–26th May 1974) p. 55.

33 op. cit.

34 Dan Danielson, 'Charismatic renewal and social concern' *Post-American* February 1975 p. 25.

35 W. J. Hollenweger, *Pentecost Between Black and White* (Belfast, Christian Journals, 1974).

36 *One World* 38 July-August 1978 p. 18.

CHAPTER 10
Is There a New Religious Fascism?

1 The literature on fascism is enormous. See, for example, S. M. Lipset, *Political Man* (Heinemann 1969); W. Kornhauser, *The Politics of Mass Society* (Routledge and Kegan Paul 1960); Eric Fromm, *The Fear of Freedom* (Routledge and Kegan Paul 1960); N. Poulantzas, *Fascism and Dictatorship* (New Left Books 1974); Leon Trotsky, *The Struggle Against Fascism in Germany* (Penguin 1975 edn); M. Vajda, *Fascism as Mass Movement* (Alison and Busby 1976); Angelo Tasca, *The Rise of Italian Fascism* (New York, Fertig 1966).

2 Renzo de Felice, *Interpretations of Fascism*, trans. Brenda Huff Everett (Harvard University Press 1977) p. 5.

3 For Reich's views see Wilhelm Reich, *The Mass Psychology of Fascism* trans. Vincent R. Carfagno (Penguin 1975 edn). Reich's use of the term 'red fascism' is very loose and seems to refer simply to totalitarian and anti-human trends. See his *Ether, God and the Devil* (1949) p. 34. Later references to 'left-wing fascism' including its use at the 1980 Labour Party Conference at Blackpool, seem to perpetuate this loose and misleading usage. Cf. Gunther Zehm, 'Is there a left-wing fascism?' *Institute of Race Relations Newsletter*, October 1968, pp. 401–7. The term seems to have been revived by Jurgen Habermas, the Frankfurt socialist philosopher, in criticisms of some young Berlin radicals of 1968.

4 The middle class is crucial in the rise of fascism. This does not however mean that there is no working class support: see Chapter 11 on this. But Trotsky's comment stands: 'The main army of fascism still consists of the petit bourgeoisie and the new middle classes: the small artisans and shopkeepers of the cities, the petty officials, the employees, the technical personnel, the intelligentsia, the impoverished peasantry.' (*The Struggle Against Fascism in Germany*, Penguin 1975 edn. p. 92.)

5 I owe much of what follows to the writings of my friend A Sivanandan, and particularly to his *Race, Class and the State* (Institute of Race Relations 1977).

6 A. Sivanandan in *Race and Class* 17:4 (1976) p. 367.

7 De Felice, op. cit. p. 6.

8 George Jackson, *Blood in my Eye* (Penguin 1975 edn) p. 155. See also Ian Macdonald, 'Some thoughts on fascism today', *Race and Class* 16:3 (1975) pp. 295–303.

9 Carl T. Schmidt *The Corporate State in Action* (1939).

10 *Enciclopedia Italiana*, Vol. 14 (1933), art. 'Fascism'.

11 James Barr, *Fundamentalism* (SCM Press 1977).

12 David Danzig, 'The radical right and the rise of the fundamentalist minority' in *Commentary* 33 (April 1962) p. 291. Cf. Daniel Bell (ed) *The Radical Right* (New York 1963) p. 21.

13 S. M. Lipset and Earl Raab, *The Politics of Unreason: Right-Wing Extremism in America 1790–1970* (Heinemann 1971).

14 ibid. pp. 117, 118.

15 ibid. p. 123.

16 Kennett T. Jackson, *The Ku Klux Klan in the City 1915–1930* (New York, Oxford University Press 1967) p. 63.

17 Ira Rohter, Radical Rightists: an Empirical Study. PhD, Dept of Political Science, Michigan State University, 1967.

18 Lipset and Raab, op. cit. Chapter 9, pp. 338–427. See also on the Christian ultra-right in the USA, George Thayer, *The Farther Shores of Politics: The American Political Fringe Today* (Penguin 1968), Chapter 9 'The Christian Right' pp. 217–261. On the Christian ultra-right in Britain see Derrick Knight, *Beyond the Pale* (Kogan Page 1981).

19 S. M. Lipset in *The Radical Right* (ed. Bell) p. 318.

20 David Reimers *White Protestantism and the Negro* (Oxford University Press 1965) p. 25.

21 ibid. pp. 46, 50.

22 On the political views of the revivalists see W. G. McLoughlin, *Modern Revivalism: C. G. Finney to Billy Graham* (New York, 1959) See also Leonard I. Sweet, 'The view of man inherent in New Measures Revivalism', *Church History* 45:2 (1976) pp. 206–221.

23 *United Evangelical Action*, 1st May 1955.

24 For the references see J. E. Barnhart, *The Billy Graham Religion* (Mowbrays 1974).

25 Athol Gill in *The New Face of Evangelicalism* (ed. C. Rene Padilla, Hodder 1976), pp. 92–3.

26 See Hans Tiefel 'The German Lutheran Church and the rise of National Socialism' *Church History* 41:3 (1972) pp. 326–336.

27 Weidenfeld and Nicolson 1964.

28 Christopher Dawson, *Religion and the Modern State* (New York 1936) pp. 135–6.

29 Encyclical *Dilectissimo Nobis* 3rd June 1933.

30 See, as an example, the Christmas sermon preached in Solingen in 1936, printed in J. S. Conway, *The Nazi Persecution of the Churches 1933–45* (Weidenfeld and Nicolson 1968) pp. 364–5. The sermon is entirely pagan with no reference to Christ or Christianity. Instead Christmas is proclaimed as 'the feast of light of our ancestors', and Hitler is described as the one who showed the German people the way to the light. 'In this hour Adolf Hitler is our benefactor, who has overcome the winter night with its terrors for the whole people and has led us under the Swastika to a new light and a new day.'

31 Douglas Hyde, 'Catholics and the National Front', *The Month*, April 1978, pp. 111–114.

32 cited in Guenter Lewy, *The Catholic Church and Nazi Germany* (Weidenfeld and Nicolson 1964) p. 25.

33 cited in Conway op. cit. p. 103.

34 ibid. p. 109.

35 *Spearhead* October 1976.

36 From a leaflet issued at the National Front demonstration in Manchester, 24th January 1975.

37 cited in Conway, op. cit. p. 161.

38 ibid. p. 116.

39 Conway, ibid; Richard Gutteridge, *Open Thy Mouth for the Dumb: The German Evangelical Church and the Jews 1879–1950* (Blackwell, 1976) Tiefel, op cit.

40 Tiefel, op. cit. p. 330.

41 ibid, p. 331.

42 *The Interpretation of History* (1936) p. 55.

43 cited in Gutteridge, op. cit. pp. 310 n. 63. Gutteridge points out that the Synod of Barmen of 1934, while it attacked the 'German Christian' heresy, did not attack the National Socialist political order. The theological influence of Karl Barth was largely responsible for the emphasis on a transcendent other-worldly Christology. Eberhard Bethge admitted that this position taken at Barmen aided the growth of a ghetto existence and the perpetuation of the 'two kingdoms' doctrine. See Gutteridge p. 148 n. 103.

44 *Letters and Papers from Prison* (1962 edn) p. 95.

45 On Kittel see Gutteridge op. cit p. 112.

46 Edwin Robertson in Dietrich Bonhoeffer, *Christology* (Fontana edn 1971) p. 21.

47 See Stuart Hall, *Drifting into a Law and Order Society* (Cobden Trust 1980); Carol Ackroyd et al. *The Technology of Political Control* (Penguin 1977); Martin Kettle and Tony Bunyan, 'The police force of the future is now here', *New Society*, 21st August 1980 pp. 351–4; Peter Hain (ed.) *Policing the Police* Vol 2 (John Calder 1980). See also the bulletin *State Research* obtainable from 9 Poland Street, London W1.

48 There is considerable evidence that Ireland is being used as a laboratory for the development of techniques soon to be used at home. See *The New Technology of Repression: Lessons from Ireland* (British Society for Social Responsibility in Science, 1974).

49 Julius Gould et al. *The Attack on Higher Education: Marxist and Radical Penetration* (Institute for the Study of Conflict 1977). For a good critique of this report see *The Attack on Higher Education – Where does it come from?* (Council for Academic Freedom and Democracy 1977).

50 See John Downing, *Now You Do Know* (War on Want 1980) for an account of racism in British society.

51 Granada TV 30th January 1978.

52 It is ironical that one publication which does (incorrectly) include the NAFF under the heading 'Fascism' alongside the NF, National Party and Column 88 is Kenneth Sloan, *Public Order and the Police* (Police Reiew 1978). Sloan does add the disclaimer: 'NAFF is only fascist in that its members are extreme right wing and oppose communism'

53 This is not a wild piece of fantasy but receives support from a number of social scientists. Cf. R. E. Pahl and J. T. Winkler, 'The coming corporatism', *New Society* 10th October 1974 pp. 72–76, describe corporatism as 'fascism with a human face.'
Cf. also Stephen Yeo in *Agenda for Prophets* (ed. David Haslam and Rex Ambler, Bowerdean Press 1980) pp. 93–4:
'Just as there is an ever-diminishing freedom of manoeuvre economically for British capitalism, so too there may be diminishing freedom of manoeuvre ideologically. As the corner gets tighter and as the more accurate explanations of the sickness and the social movements behind them loom larger, we may expect increasingly shrill reaffirmations of the moralising explanation, which will offer the church and its archbishops a seductive but essentially mystifying role. False prophets will arise, looking uncommonly like a cross between Edward Heath, Mary Whitehouse, Harold Wilson and Donald Coggan. They may even assume the more sinister shape of the Revd Moon of South Korea. Organised evangelism has been getting steadily more sinister since Billy Graham, Nixon's favourite Christian. The false prophets will have the odd entertainer from the newspaper industry, the odd ex-Prime Minister and the odd board member from that well-known would-be company Great Britain Limited (motto, democracy is inefficient) at their side. Most liberals and even the odd trade union leader will rally round. If exhortation does not work, "sterner measures" will be applied. I will be dismissed as paranoid but I am serious in saying that this is the soil from which a mutant of fascism can grow, and can be supported by good Christians.'

54 See Margaret Thatcher, 'I Believe: A speech on Christianity and Politics,' St Lawrence Jewry, 30th March 1978, Conservative Central Office News Service 442/78. On the theological aspects of Thatcherism see John Atherton, 'The theological critique of Thatcherism' in *Thatcherism: A Christian Critique* (ed. Kenneth Leech, Jubilee Group 1980).

55 *Christian Newsletter Supplement* 11, 10th January 1940.

56 E. L. Mascall, *The Secularisation of Christianity* (Darton, Longman and Todd, 1965) p. 7.

57 This is discussed in various essays in *Agenda for Prophets* op. cit.

58 See Chapter 1.

59 See my *Youthquake* (Sheldon Press 1972) pp. 165–170.

60 *The Modern Churchman* 16:1 (October 1972).

61 See O. R. Johnston, *Christianity in a collapsing culture* (Exeter, Paternoster Press 1976). This is worth careful scrutiny for its indication of the concerns and the style of argument adopted by the Festival of Light.

62 See, for many examples of this technique, her *Whatever Happened to Sex?* (Wayland Publishers 1977).

63 Max Caulfield, *Mary Whitehouse* (1975) p. 35.

64 cited in Tom Driberg, *The Mystery of Moral Rearmament* (Secker and Warburg 1964) p. 68.

65 *The Open Secret of MRA* (Blandford Press 1964) pp. 59–66.

66 *The Defender*, 15th March 1935 cited in Gustavus Myers, *History of Bigotry in the United States* (New York Capricorn 1960) p. 367.

67 See for example, John Tyndall's open letter to clergy critics of the National Front in *Spearhead* December 1977.

CHAPTER 11
The Local Roots of Fascism

1 Cf. Colin Sparks, *Never Again! The hows and whys of stopping fascism* (Bookmarks 1980) p. 31: 'In terms of its ideology, social composition, strategy and tactics fascism is the logical expression of the middle class in a period of capitalist crisis.' See also his 'Fascism and the working class: the German experience'. *International Socialism* 2:2 (Autumn 1978) pp. 41–69. Many writers in the 1930s and '40s stressed the appeal of fascism to the threatened middle class and to the suburban populations. Cf. J. H. Oldham, *Christian Newsletter*, 7th May 1941, Supplement 80, 'The Nazi Creed; its links with Prussia and nihilism': 'The Hitler movement is suburban, and suburbia is everywhere practically out of touch with the traditions of Europe, including its religious traditions. There were therefore no resources available that could have provided the power of resistance once the Nazi creed began to sway the despairing masses of Germany . . . If anybody should doubt the statement that the Nazi movement is suburban and therefore out of touch with any traditional element of our civilisation, let him read *Mein Kampf*. There you find the wild verbosity of a half-educated man, fed on newspapers and swayed by headlines. There is in the whole book not a glimpse of any conviction nourished by one of the sources of our

tradition. It is all newspaper trash passionately absorbed by an unguided mind. This formidable man belongs to nowhere in spite of all his boisterous nationalist talk. He has no roots, he is a citizen of suburbia.'

2 On this campaign see L. P. Gartner, *The Jewish Immigrant in England 1870–1914* (Allen and Unwin 1960); J. A. Garrard, *The English and Immigration* (Institute of Race Relations and Oxford University Press 1971); and, for contemporary accounts, Arnold White (ed.) *The Destitute Alien in Great Britain* (Swan, Sonnerschein, 1892); W. Evans-Gordon, *The Alien Immigrant* (Heinemann 1903); M. J. Landa, *The Alien Problem and its Remedy* (P. S. King, 1911)

3 For a comparison see Caroline Adams, *They Sell Cheaper and They Live Very Odd* (British Council of Churches 1976).

4 See Paul Foot, *Immigration and Race in British Politics* (Penguin 1965).

5 J. H. Robb *Working Class Anti-Semite* (Tavistock 1954). The reputation of Bethnal Green as a district hostile to the Jews was well-established in the early years of the century. Cf. Jerry White, *Rothschild Buildings: Life in an East End Tenement Block 1887–1920* (Routledge and Kegan Paul 1980) p. 136: 'There was one part of the East End, however, which had a consistently threatening reputation for the people of Rothschild Buildings. This was Bethnal Green.' One former resident whom White interviewed recalled: 'Bethnal Green was a Christian area and we avoided it because we were afraid of being beaten up. I remember a friend of my mother's coming up to us with his hat all bashed in. And he had been attacked at the end of Brick Lane going towards Bethnal Green. I remember somebody saying, "Well, why did you go that way?" He should have gone another way to avoid Bethnal Green. It had a very bad name.' (ibid.)

6 On the fascist movement in the East End in the 1930s see Robin Benewick, *Political Violence and Public Order* (Penguin 1969); Colin Cross, *The Fascists in Britain* (Barrie and Rockliff 1961); Phil Piratin *Our Flag Stays Red* (Thames Publications 1948; revised edition, Lawrence and Wishart 1978); Joe Jacobs, *Out of the Ghetto: My Youth in the East End, Communism and Fascism 1913–1939* (Janet Simon, 29 Troutbeck, Albany Street, London NW1, 1978); Joe Jacobs, 'The police and the fascists: East London 1932–36', *Race Today*, December 1973, pp. 341–2; Colin Sparks, 'Fighting the beast: fascism: the lessons of Cable Street', *International Socialism* 94 (January 1977) pp. 11–14; Caroline Knowles, 'Labour and anti-semitism: an account of the political discourse surrounding the Labour Party's involvement with anti-semitism in East London 1934–6' in *Racism and Political Action in Britain* (ed. Robert Miles and Annie Phizacklea, Routledge and Kegan Paul 1979) pp. 50–71; and many other books and papers.

7 See Michael Banton, *The Coloured Quarter* (Cape 1955): the title is very misleading, for Cable Street never was a 'coloured quarter' in any strict sense of that term.

8 *East London Advertiser*, 17th October 1947.

9 ibid 30th May 1958.

10 *Combat*, March-April 1961, pp. 1 and 7.

11 See Stan Taylor, 'The National Front: anatomy of a political movement' in Miles and Phizacklea op. cit. pp. 124–146; and Christopher T. Husbands. 'The "threat" hypothesis and racist voting in England and the United States' in ibid. pp. 147–183; D. Scott, 'The National Front in local politics: some interpretations' in *British Political Sociology Yearbook*, Vol 2. *The Politics of Race* (ed. I. Crewe, Croom Helm 1975) pp. 214–238.

12 See Paul Whiteley, 'The National Front vote in the 1977 GLC elections: an aggregate data analysis', *British Journal of Political Science* 9:3 (July 1979) pp. 370–380.

13 See my pamphlet *Brick Lane 1978: The events and their significance* (Birmingham, AFFOR 1980) for a detailed treatment.

14 *The Guardian*, 9th December 1977.

15 *Blood on the Streets* (Tower Hamlets Trades Council 1978). See also *Brick Lane: the case for the defence* (Tower Hamlets Trades Council, 1979).

16 *East Ender*, 21st July 1978.

17 See Christopher T. Husbands and Jude England 'The hidden support for racism' *New Statesman*, 11th May 1978; Michael Steed 'The National Front vote' *Parliamentary Affairs* 31 (1978) pp. 282–293; Christopher T. Husbands, 'The National Front: what happens to it now?' *Marxism Today* September 1979, pp. 268–275.

18 Martin Walker *The National Front* (Fontana 1977).

19 M. Harrop and G. Zimmerman. 'The National Front' American Political Science Association. *British Politics Group Newsletter* 10 (Fall 1977), and 'The anatomy of the National Front' (Department of Politics, University of Essex).

20 Whiteley's analysis of the 1977 GLC voting data shows that the north-eastern area of London (i.e. the area including the East End and Hoxton) had a 3.26 per cent higher vote for the National Front than the rest of London. His work supports the view of Husbands that a distinctive East End political culture is central here. Drawing on the study by Gareth Stedman Jones, Husbands argues that the economic role of the metropolis fostered the growth of casualism in the East End and militated against the development of a disciplined and organised working class. 'London's East End was for a long time intractable to penetration by working-class-based political parties, and it preferred Conservative paternalism till well into the present century.' (Husbands in Miles and Phizacklea op. cit. p. 175.) See also Gareth Stedman Jones, *Outcast London* (Penguin 1976).

On the wider question of working class support for fascism, there is now a considerable literature on Nazi Germany and the appeal of the Hitler movement to the working-class. For a summary of recent research see Detlef Muhlberger, 'The sociology of the NSDAP: the question of working class membership', *Journal of Contemporary History* 15:3 (July 1980) pp. 493–511.

21 *Spearhead* 79, September-October 1974, p. 11.

22 Letter in *The Times*, 22nd August 1977.

23 G. Weightman and S. Weir, 'The National Front and the young: a

special survey', *New Society* 27th April 1978, pp. 186–193.

24 *Spearhead* 85, July 1975, p. 17. But Stan Taylor, 'The incidence of coloured populations and support for the National Front', *British Journal of Political Science* 9:2 (April 1979) pp. 250–255, has argued that there is no clear evidence of a correlation between the presence of black people and the support for the Front.

25 cited in Walker, op. cit. p. 145.

26 *The Observer*, 11th September 1977.

CHAPTER 12
Theological Renewal and the Catholic Left

1 See Stuart Hall in *Marxism Today*, January 1979, pp. 14–20.

2 E. R. Norman, *Christianity and the World Order* (Oxford, 1979). See also Kenneth Leech (ed) *Christianity Reinterpreted? A Critical Examination of the 1978 Reith Lectures* (Church in Wales Publications, 1979).

3 Helder Camara, 'What would St Thomas Aquinas, the Aristotle commentator, do if faced with Karl Marx?' in *Celebrating the Medieval Heritage: A Colloquy on the Thought of Aquinas and Bonaventure* edited by David Tracy, *The Journal of Religion*, Vol. 58, Supplement, 1978, University of Chicago.

4 See Jon Sobrino, 'Christian Prayer and New Testament Theology: A Basis for Social Justice and Spirituality' in Matthew Fox (ed) *Western Spirituality: Historical Roots, Ecumenical Routes* (Notre Dame, Indiana, Fides/Claretian, 1979) pp. 76–114.

5 Westminster Press, Philadelphia, 1972.

6 See Vladimir Lossky, *The Mystical Theology of the Eastern Church* (1955).

7 John Hick (ed) *The Myth of God Incarnate* (SCM Press 1977).

8 E. R. Norman, op. cit. p. 77.

9 Henri Nouwen, 'Pentecostalism on Campus' in *Intimacy* (Notre Dame, Fides, 1969) pp. 63–76.

10 Norman, op. cit. pp. 2, 78.

11 See P. H. Connell, 'Ether drinking in Ulster', *Quarterly Journal of Studies in Alcoholism*, Vol. 26 (1965) pp. 629–653.

12 See E. P. Thompson, *The Poverty of Theory and Other Essays* (Merlin 1978) for a critique of Althusser's 'theoretical anti-humanism.'

13 See Sheila Rowbotham, Lynn Segal and Hilary Wainwright, *Beyond the Fragments* (Merlin 1979).

14 John Lewis, *Marxism and the Open Mind* (Routledge and Kegan Paul, 1957).

15 On the theology of nature and grace see Roger Haight, *The Experience and Language of Grace* (Gill and Macmillan, 1979).

16 J. L. Segundo, *The Liberation of Theology* (Maryknoll, Orbis, 1976) pp. 140–141.

17 Reinhold Niebuhr, *The Nature and Destiny of Man*, cited and criticised by Chris Sugden, 'The Kingdom and the kingdoms', *Third Way*, 30th June 1977, p. 8.

18 *Catholic Crusader* 16, January 1933, p. 3.

19 Conrad Noel, *Jesus the Heretic* (Dent 1939) pp. 219–220.

20 On the Song of Songs, cited in Thomas Hopko, *The Spirit of God* (Wilton, Conn, Morehouse-Barlow, 1976) pp. ii-iii.

21 Georges Florovsky, *Creation and Redemption*, *Collected Works*, Vol 3 (Belmont, Mass. Nordland Publishing Company, 1976) p. 98.

22 On Nietzsche and fascism scc Alistair Kee, 'A Christian critique of fascism' in *The Modern Churchman* 22:2–3 (Summer 1979) pp 74–85.

23 *Redemptor Hominis*, 4th March 1979 para. 16.

24 Gregory Baum, *The Social Imperative* (Paulist Press 1979) pp. 5, 30.

25 Douglas Johnson (ed) *A Brief History of the International Fellowship of Evangelical Students* (Inter Varsity Fellowship, 1964) p. 177.

26 Lakeland 1975. Reviewing this book in *The Churchman*, John Gladwyn, one of the leaders of evangelical social thinking in the Church of England, described it as 'ill-defined to the point of illiteracy' and its politics 'that of the illiterate right'. See John Gladwyn, 'Social involvement and evangelism', *The Churchman* 89:4 (October-December 1975) p. 292.
Classical Pentecostalism has been sadly lacking in any theology of society. Cf. Robert Mapes Anderson, *Vision of the Disinherited: The Making of American Pentecostalism* (New York, Oxford University Press 1979) p. 201: 'Not society but the individual, not reform but escape – that has been the heart of Pentecostal social theory.'

27 *The Christian in Industrial Society* (1964) p. 32.

28 Catholic Renewal in the Church of England, Loughborough *Conference Report* (Church Literature Association September 1979) p. 33.

29 cited in the Bishop of Chichester's Presidential Address to the Church Union, 6th December 1976.

Index